The
Clutter–Busting
Handbook
ೞ ❖ ೞ

ALSO BY RITA EMMETT

The Procrastinator's Handbook

The Procrastinating Child

THE
CLUTTER-BUSTING

HANDBOOK

Clean It Up, Clear It Out, and Keep
Your Life Clutter-Free

Rita Emmett

Anchor Canada

Library and Archives Canada Cataloguing in Publication has been applied for.

Book design by M.J. DiMassi
Illustrations by Helen Flook
Book composition by Coghill Composition Company
Printed and bound in Canada

Published in Canada by
Anchor Canada, a division of
Random House of Canada Limited

Visit Random House of Canada Limited's website: www.randomhouse.ca

TRANS   10 9 8 7 6 5 4 3 2 1

This book is dedicated to two groups:

First, to those clutter collectors who feel there is no hope for their mounds of jumbled stuff. May this book bring you relief, help, and hope.

Second, to my husband's and my friends and family, including our kids, kids-in-law, and our nine glorious grandchildren, who are shining lights of endless delight, and to Bruce Karder, husband, business partner, lover, wind beneath my wings, goofy guy, adviser, greatest supporter, best friend, and—alas—King of Klutter.

Contents

INTRODUCTION ix

Part I: When Enough Becomes Too Much

1: How Did I Accumulate All This Stuff? 3

2: Gonna Take a Sentimental Journey 31

Part II: Get Rid of Clutter and Keep It Out

3: Fifty Ways to Leave Your Clutter 55

4: How to Start? Work It Smart 70

5: Caution! Incoming Stealth Clutter 88

6: How to Handle Paper and Computer Info-Clutter 109

7: Home Sweet Clutter-Busted Home 136

8: Caged Clutter—Out of Sight and Out of My Mind 154

9: The Joy to Be Clutter-Free 171

ACKNOWLEDGMENTS 181

INDEX 185

Introduction

Years ago, my best friend would never walk into my house because the clutter all over my kitchen counters and floors made her nervous. One day she offered to come over and help me sort through and get rid of all that mess. The first thing she picked up was a coupon for fifteen cents off a box of cereal. The coupon had expired over eighteen months earlier. She set it down, picked up her purse, and said, "Rita, let's go to my house and have a cup of coffee."

As a "Recovered Pack Rat," I am writing this book to pass on to you what I've learned, as well as tips from other people who are working on their clutter. To protect the privacy of those who have contributed their stories, I've used first names and composites.

People of all ages, occupations, educational levels, and geographic locations suffer from clutter. And they all tend to ask the same questions and have a strong need to understand: *How does clutter accumulate so fast? Is there any way to get rid of it that is easy and painless?*

Several years ago I wrote a book about how to stop procrastinating. Many readers e-mailed to tell me that they were grateful for the book and that it helped them become procrastination-free. They often went on to ask, "*Now* what do I do about the clutter in my life?"

Clutter is a chief source of stress, headaches, embarrassment, and anxiety these days. Recently I asked a question about clutter in my e-zine, sent it out, then left on a four-day trip. When I returned, my e-mail account was jammed with hundreds of responses, all eager to tell me their "Frustrating Clutter Stories." These stories ranged from family battles over clutter to terrible conflicts at work due to papers lost "somewhere in the office." Sidetracked dreams, lost treasures, stress, guilt, and anxiety were all common themes among these tales of clutter woe. And all of the respondents begged for advice on conquering the clutter that seemed to be overtaking their lives.

Throughout this book, you'll find advice, anecdotes, tips, and quizzes to help you more clearly identify the what, where, how, and why of your clutter, and thereby gain a better grasp of your specific clutter situation. You will see that:

- Clutter is just a habit—one you can break.
- There is a definite connection between clutter and procrastination.
- There are many gentle (not heart-wrenching) ways to get rid of your clutter.

- Once you clutter-bust, not only is it easier to find *places* for your remaining stuff, but it is easier to *find* your remaining stuff.
- There are steps you can take to keep clutter from returning.

Once you have conquered your clutter, you'll be amazed at how terrific it is to feel in control of your belongings instead of vice versa; you have more energy and space, fewer distractions and anxieties. You can't imagine how light and fantastic you will feel when you are free of all that is cluttering up your life.

Part I

❦❦◆❦❦

When Enough
Becomes Too Much

1

How Did I Accumulate All This Stuff?

Life is not a having and getting,
but a being and a doing.
—anonymous

Dear Rita, the Clutter Buster,

We came home recently to find police cars at our house. We'd been burglarized and before going into the house, a police officer took me aside and said, "Let me warn you: These thugs totally trashed your house. Tell your wife to brace herself. It will take you weeks to clear up the mess they made."

So we went in, looked around, and the thieves hadn't touched a thing. Everything was just the way we left it. What the cop thought was "the mess they made" is just the way we live.

I love all my stuff and have argued that it isn't clutter, but deep down always knew that it was. Now I have to admit it does seem that something is wrong here—my stuff is out of control. I'm possibly the most disorganized person in the world, and I've promised that tomorrow I've got to get organized . . . but I'm discouraged and don't really believe there's hope for me. Is there?

Sincerely,

Overwhelmed, in Oshkosh, Wisconsin

Yes, there is hope.

Being surrounded with clutter is not a personality flaw or a character trait; it's a habit you can learn to break. Actually, clutter stems from four bad habits, which I call the Deadly Sins of Clutter. Do you:

- **S**ave everything (whether you need it or want it or not)?
- **I**nsist on bringing home (or allowing into your home) stuff you don't need?
- **N**ever assign a place where each thing belongs?
- **S**et things aside or drop them, intending "to put them away later"?

The first two habits account for how clutter comes into your life and doesn't leave. The last two represent a failure to follow the adage "A place for everything, and everything in its place." If you have any or all of these habits, you've got clutter. Breaking even just one of these habits will automatically decrease your clutter.

You might say, "Wait a minute! My clutter doesn't come from those Deadly Sins. It comes from being disorganized."

> ### TOO TRUE TO ARGUE
> Emmett's Basic Clutter Fact: If you plan to get organized tomorrow, you've got to de-clutter today.
> Getting organized when you're surrounded by clutter is so difficult, it's almost impossible. But getting organized once your clutter is gone is almost effortless.

Understand this: Whether you are organized or not, if you stopped each of these four Deadly Sins of Clutter, your clutter would disappear.

Webster's New World College Dictionary defines *clutter* as "a number of things scattered in a disordered jumble." However, two people might disagree on what is a disordered jumble. I think stuff becomes clutter when:

- It creates problems, stress, or embarrassment.
- You don't know what you have or can't find what you have.
- It keeps you from using an area, place, or thing for its intended purpose.
- It impairs your ability to function.

The Dining-Room-Table File System

Before I converted from my cluttered way of living, I bragged that we were a casual, informal family who preferred to eat our meals in the kitchen instead of the dining room. The true story was that my dining room table was stacked so high with papers, books, and stuff, it would have taken me hours to clear it off.

I was embarrassed by the mess, and when company came, I'd scoop everything into a box and stash it in a closet. That would create total chaos later because we'd lose track of everything in the box. Often bills or important papers were misplaced or forgotten because they were buried on that dining room table or in a closet.

Like many people, I was "clutter numb"—I didn't notice clutter as it piled up until there was too much to ignore.

WE ARE THE CLUTTER GENERATION

Never in the history of the world has any generation been as overwhelmed with stuff and clutter as we are. Which generation do I mean? All of us. Whether you are a great-grandparent or a preteen or anyone in between, you have piles more stuff than any great-grandparent or preteen from years gone by.

According to the Avery newsletter *Great Results,* the average three-bedroom house today contains approximately 350,000 items. What a contrast to the olden days, when a family could pack up everything they owned into a cart or wagon to travel to another place.

A century ago, most people probably could not imagine why anyone would ever need four or five pairs of shoes, eight pairs of pants, or ten dresses. Just a generation or two ago, even the wealthy didn't possess nearly the amount of printed material that today's average household owns. Back then, it was a lot easier to find a place to put everything because there were not that many things to put away.

In one of my "clutter-busting seminars," Brad, a father of three, said that his grandmother used to tell stories of how thrilled she was as a little girl when her father carved a wooden horse for her birthday gift. Brad went on to say that many children today have more toys than they could ever play with, and most would not be excited if all they received was one handmade toy for their birthday.

Another big difference is that most members of the generations before us lived by the adage "Don't replace it. Repair it." My parents certainly preached that, but the advice hardly applies today. It's not possible to repair many of the appliances that have computer chips in them, and even when you take something in to be repaired, the person you deal with may well tell you that it would be a lot cheaper to buy a new one.

Generations before us had much less stuff pouring into their lives. Here's a quote from *Good Housekeeping*, August 1952: "Your possessions express your personality. Few things, including clothes, are more personal than your cherished ornaments. The pioneer women, who crossed a wild continent clutching their treasures to them, knew that a clock, a picture, a pair of candlesticks, meant home, even in the wilderness." What do all our possessions today express about our personalities?

During a seminar, a speaker recently claimed, "Research says that today's generation never uses 80 percent of what we keep." I don't know the source of that research, but based on my observations, I believe it to be true for most of us. When you feel swamped or overwhelmed by your things or papers, realize that because your parents never had to handle this kind of clutter, you probably were never taught any clutter-management skills.

DON'T MESS WITH MY MESS

Many people are like the letter writer at the beginning of this chapter; for them, clutter is so much a part of their lifestyle, they seem unaware of it. They become so accustomed to their clutter, they don't realize how much time and energy they spend searching through it, stepping over it, walking around it, and trying to ignore it.

When this clutter is brought to their attention, they may defiantly declare, "Don't mess with my mess!" They claim that no matter how big the jumble, they can immediately find whatever it is they are looking for. But nine out of ten times, they're kidding themselves. They block out of their memories all the time spent shuffling and searching, all the stress, headaches, and anxiety as they frantically look for something they need fast that keeps eluding them, and all the things that are never, ever located when needed.

"A You've Got Clutter" Quiz

What's your favorite reason for holding on to an item?

> A. It's good as new.
> B. It's too good to throw out.
> C. It might be useful someday.
> D. It might be valuable someday.
> E. It's inherited or was received as a loving gift from someone.
> F. It's part of a collection.
> G. Somebody else might need it . . . someday.
> H. I'm going to fix it or find a use for it someday.
> I. Nothing should ever, ever, ever be thrown away!
> J. All of the above.

If you selected three or more of these statements, you need to work on the first Deadly Sin, "Save everything (whether you need it or want it or not)."

CAGED AND WILD CLUTTER

Have you ever heard a great tip to get rid of clutter, and when you tried it, it didn't work? Either the tip didn't make the clut-

ter go away, or the clutter went away only to return a week later.

I think I've discovered why some clutter tips just don't work. In reality, there are two types of clutter—and they require different kinds of strategies. Like jungle animals, clutter can be "wild" or "caged."

Caged clutter is usually out of sight, and like an animal, when clutter is in its "cage," it tends to be contained and "under control" (though not completely). For example, when you don't know where to put something, you put it in a place designated to hold clutter—a desk junk drawer, perhaps, or a kitchen "hell drawer." Other spots for caged clutter include:

- files
- an "in box"
- under the bed
- attic or crawl space
- garage
- basement
- a spare room

In contrast to caged clutter, wild clutter accumulates right out in the open, where it bugs you, embarrasses you, or makes you crazy. Things slither into places they don't belong, usually someplace right in front of your face like your desk, dining room table, or bedroom floor.

There are lots of other places wild clutter can accumulate. For example:

- kitchen counters
- tops of file cabinets
- inside vehicles
- coffee tables
- purses and wallets
- office floors
- tops of refrigerators
- nightstands
- corners of rooms

Wild clutter has no boundaries; it prowls and roams wherever it pleases, and like that jungle animal, it's more potentially dangerous than caged clutter. In this case, because it causes more stress, guilt, and anxiety.

A caged-clutter tip might not work on wild clutter. For instance, a tip to put things in containers makes sense for caged clutter (such as your garage clutter or your junk-drawer clutter). But if your bedroom or office floor is strewn with tons of junky clutter, bringing several containers into the room may just compound the problem. Besides, you don't have a clue what you'll be finding in that stack of clutter, so how would you even know what kind of containers to get? Or how many?

The Pitfalls of Procrastination Plateaus

Both wild and caged clutter often result from procrastination. Take a look at that accumulation on your dining room table, your kitchen counters, or your desk. Many times the clutter is the result of your screeching to a halt at one of these Procrastination Plateaus.

1. The "Will I Keep This?" Plateau: "I can't decide whether I want to keep this or not. So I'll set it down here for just a minute and I'll decide later."

2. The "Where Will I Put This?" Plateau: "Well, I've decided that I *am* going to keep this, but now I can't decide *where* to keep it. So I'll set it down here for just a minute and I'll decide later." Or the equally insidious "How Will I Get Rid of This?" Plateau: "Well, I've decided that I'm *not* going to keep this, but

now I can't decide how to get rid of it. So I'll set it . . ." You know the drill.

3. The "I'm *So* Exhausted" Plateau: "Well, I've decided to keep it *and* I've decided where to put it. But I'm just too exhausted to put it there. So I'll set it down here for just a minute and put it away later."

If you stop on any of the plateaus—ka-boom! You've got clutter. The solution is to recognize when you are pausing on one of these plateaus, and that putting off decisions leads to clutter. Most of the time, simply realizing that you have hit a Procrastination Plateau is all you need to counterattack those "I'll do it later" episodes, and scramble off that plateau right then and there. No matter which plateau you are on, the solution is the same one you've heard all your life: Do it now. What is new and the real key is to add: *Decide It Now.*

Is Clutter Ever Tame?
(Hint: This Is a Trick Question)

Alas, my metaphor limps in one regard. With animals, there is a third category. Besides wild and caged, there are *tame* animals, which we call pets. The term does not apply to clutter because once your clutter is tamed, it's no longer clutter.

Consider, for example, Georgia's experience with clutter. While she was growing up, her mother had often told her that everybody has a "hell drawer" in their kitchen, overflowing with junky, useless stuff that they cannot throw out. Georgia believed this was true until one day about three years ago, when she bought a big box of little containers at a garage sale. She went home, ran them through the dishwasher (because they were dusty and grungy), then went through the house looking for places that needed little containers, places that contained caged clutter.

She emptied everything out of her hell drawer and sorted items by category, putting all the rubber bands in one little square container, all the pens in a rectangular container, the thumbtacks in a round one, and so forth. Then she threw out probably half of what was in there—because Georgia finally admitted she had no use for it and probably never would. (To this day, she doesn't know what she planned to do with a million itty-bitty pieces of string, and thirty-seven smashed bows from holiday gifts.)

Suddenly, her caged clutter was tamed. And it's been fairly easy for Georgia and her son Ricky to put items back into their designated containers. Georgia's hell drawer no longer makes her feel guilty or crazy or stupid or messy or sloppy or like "Tomorrow I've *got* to get organized." In truth, it's no longer a hell drawer.

Once clutter is tamed and stays tamed, it is no longer clutter.

TYPES OF CLUTTERERS

Most people have some sort of clutter in their lives at one time or another, and you'll probably recognize yourself in one of these categories,* depending on the amount of clutter you accumulate.

Clutter Glutton

You are a Clutter Glutton if you collect too much stuff for your living or working space and have a hard time getting rid of things, but you try to keep clutter under control by establishing more cages for it. Sometimes, when you survey all your accumulations, you are "clutter numb" and just don't *see* how cluttered your surroundings are. But eventually the time comes when you recognize what a mess you are in and experience a range of emotions:

- You feel swamped or overwhelmed by all your belongings.
- You are filled with anxiety, guilt, and stress.
- You regret the lost and wasted time spent giving space to, caring for, and rummaging through your stuff.

At that point you may decide to put an end to the chaos and begin a frenzied clutter-busting spree.

---

*These categories are for behaviors of people with some degree of good mental health and do not include the Compulsive Hoarder, a third category. Compulsive hoarding is a little-understood behavior usually requiring professional counseling.

The Pack Rat

The Pack Rat has more extreme clutter. If you are one, you bring home, collect, and save a wide assortment of ordinary or wonderfully weird items. Not only do you have no earthly use for these items, but you do not want to get rid of any of them . . . not ever.

If you're a Pack Rat, you know that you're not highly functional. You lose important information, and you miss deadlines. You say, "I didn't have time to do that," but deep in your heart you know you actually forget to do things because your mind is overwhelmed with all the stuff piled around you. You lose invitations or other information telling you the time and place of business and social appointments. You often think, "Someday I've got to get organized," but it never happens.

TOO TRUE TO ARGUE

Emmett's Third Clutter Fact: When you have chaos and clutter in your work or living space, you have chaos and clutter in your mind and in your heart.
When clutter surrounds you, your mind becomes jumbled; it's hard to focus, hard to establish priorities and decide what you should be taking care of first, hard to think clearly or to even know what you feel.

When you stop and view all your clutter, you come up with a million rationalizations and excuses for why you should keep every single thing. You truly believe you or somebody else will use these items someday, and it breaks your heart to throw away perfectly good stuff that someone somewhere somehow someday might find a use for.

It takes a lot for a Pack Rat to start getting rid of stuff. Most often what moves you to this point is not an internal awareness but an external circumstance such as company coming, the need for more room, the necessity to find something important among the clutter, or your spouse threatening divorce or murder.

WHAT'S YOUR CLUTTER STYLE?

There are many methods people employ to bring clutter into their lives. Some are shared by everyone and some are unique. Whether you are a clutter glutton or the more extreme Pack Rat, you'll probably recognize at least one of these many styles of accumulating clutter.

The Shopper

You shop as if a giant vacuum cleaner is sucking every item in sight right into your hands or shopping cart. If an item is on sale, you'll buy not one but a dozen. You can come up with plenty of reasons for making this purchase, but the main one is that it was a good deal.

The Receiver

When Jim's friends and acquaintances de-cluttered, they would come across stacks of junk that was just too good to throw out. Jim wondered if he had *Receiver* tattooed across his forehead, because everyone gave him their hand-me-downs, castoffs, and just plain junk.

The weird thing was, as Jim looks back on it, he actually encouraged that behavior because he always would act delighted to receive the other person's trash and he'd happily tell him or her that he could use it all. While the other people got rid of clutter, he added to his; then he would feel frustrated and embarrassed about all the clutter in his home and office.

Over time, Jim learned how to stop being a Receiver. It's not that hard, and if this is your clutter style, you can do the same. This book will give you step-by-step directions.

CULTIVATE A SIMPLE HABIT

When people are dumping their clutter
And offer to give it to you,
No matter how much that you want it,
You *know* what's the right thing to do.

'Cause furniture, books, and old clothing
Are things they're delighted to give,
But don't bring home *any* items
Unless they have someplace to live.

The Crusader Collector

You do not collect only beautiful, valuable, or rare items. No, you'll usually collect anything and everything: broken toasters, rubber bands, chewed-up pencils, cars that don't work. You are sensational at seeing the potential in the lowliest of things. Unfortunately, those things never seem to realize their potential, but you keep them anyway.

The Duplicator

Have you ever, during a clutter-busting session, been shocked to discover that you had several of the same item for no apparent reason? Long ago, while cleaning out my kitchen cabinets, I came across *nine* bottles of green food color. And I had used only a couple of drops from each.

Before Deb conquered her clutter, the ritual at her house, when they couldn't find what they needed "right now," was to go out and buy another. Then they were constantly finding duplicates of the oddest things. She remembers one evening when she, her husband, and their son were sorting through some boxes they found in the basement. They came across twelve eyeglass cases (nobody in the house wears glasses) and five copies of *John Denver and the Muppets Celebrate Christmas*. Nobody could explain why one family would own all that.

The Hobbyist

People have all kinds of hobbies. Some hobbies, like carpentry and sewing, are practical, while others, such as whittling toothpicks out of chunks of wood, are not. But people are passionate about their hobbies and will tell you that while working on them they lose track of time, and what they're doing never feels like work.

Hobbyists collect and accumulate all sorts of supplies, equipment, books, and tools. These fabrics, metals, beads, threads, wax, glass, paints, chunks of wood, et cetera often are odd sizes and shapes, and cannot be made to look neat or uniform. (What do you pack a telescope into?)

Renee's husband has a whole room of their house filled with his model trains. Why? "Because our children decided to grow up and move out," she explained. "Also because he's married to a woman kind enough to give up her cherished guest room for teeny, tiny towns that his trains run through." Most people don't have the luxury of a whole room for their hobby.

It's wonderful if you have a cabinet or closet for your paraphernalia, but often you can't devote an entire area to your accumulation. Many crafters have the habit of once a year getting rid of unused beads, fabric, and other items, aware that they will start to gather more in no time. Otherwise, they often end up tucking thee things away and forgetting about them anyway. To have a regular system of giving away some of your stuff forces you to "take inventory" once in a while.

One important tip for organizing your hobby: Keep similar items together, and if it's possible to box them up, label the boxes with as much detailed explanation as possible. True, you can't pack up everything—that stationary bike is a bit cumbersome to stuff in a box—but the more you can make things look neat, the less cluttered you will feel.

Another good tip is to set boundaries on your beloved accumulations. When the yarn or drawings or tiles or glass or whatever reach a certain level, stop collecting and start disposing. You know in your heart that in the blink of an eye, more will come your way.

The Caregiver

Carol used to buy things she didn't need but thought a family member, friend, or coworker might need someday. She finally stopped that behavior after taking a few minutes to really think about what she was doing. If somebody ever did need what she had bought, she would have forgotten she had it because it would be buried under all the clutter. And if she did remember that she had it, she had to be honest and admit that she would never know where to start looking for it, and nine times out of ten, she could not find what the person needed.

All the stuff she was saving was just sitting there doing no good for anyone. So Carol decided that if she really wanted to take care of people, she would donate all those items to her church when it had a drive to help the poor. That way Carol's

Jobs That Promote Clutter

Many people work in fields that promote and generate stuff that might look like clutter but is necessary to the profession. Examples include sales (especially with samples and promotional products), art, publishing, tailoring/sewing, carpentry, landscaping, decorating, writing, designing, and floristry.

Madeline, after working in nonprofit companies for two decades, became a high-school teacher a few years ago. She was amazed by the amount of teacher-related materials she had to make room for at home, adding to clutter from her previous jobs and the usual household accumulations.

Your line of work can have a tremendous impact on your home clutter. In order to be professional and do a superior job, you might *have* to accumulate a lot of stuff. Then, because you sometimes work at home or think about work-related things at home (or maybe you ran out of room at work), you start to bring stuff home.

The situation gets compounded if you leave one job, bring home all that you've collected over the years, then switch careers but feel you must keep everything from the first place just in case you decide to return to that original occupation. Now you have all the usual household clutter, plus the clutter you've accrued in one, or maybe even more, of your careers. At this point, you start to feel like a giant clutter-magnet.

There's another reason why you accumulate so much. You may gather things around you because you truly love your work and want to surround yourself with work-related items in your home life. You then save them forever just because they are beautiful and they nourish your soul.

That's what Jo-Anne's mother did. She designed costumes for the Metropolitan Opera in New York and had a great eye for unusual and beautiful fabrics. She would buy a piece of cloth just because it was beautiful. Sometimes she would use it to make a cushion or a blouse, but mostly it just accumulated in a cedar chest or in boxes or on her sewing table.

For twenty years after her mother died, Jo-Anne stored that fabric, packing it up and carting it every time she moved to a new place. Finally, she decided to give it all to the Refugee Furniture Bank in Toronto, Canada, and a talented woman there turned the fabric into cushion covers, place mats, and drapes. Now many new residents of Canada are enjoying the beautiful fabrics that had been collected by Jo-Anne's mother. But think of how much time and energy packing and unpacking and how much space Jo-Anne's mother and then Jo-Anne had devoted to that fabric all those years.

If you are swamped by business-related clutter as well as personal clutter, take comfort in knowing that the clutter-busting techniques in this book apply to both types of clutter.

Three warnings for people who work in clutter-attracting fields:

1. Do not allow so much stuff to come into your work and living space that you're forced to stash away most of it to the extent that years go by without your seeing it.

2. Just because your work/creative things resemble clutter, don't give yourself permission to accumulate clutter in other areas of your life.

3. Learn to set boundaries, to limit the amount of stuff you will allow to pour into your life. Dispose of or refuse to acquire anything beyond that limit.

"caring gifts" could be distributed to people who would love and cherish them.

Now Carol can admit that she used to buy so much mainly because she enjoyed buying. Facing that truth enabled her to cut back significantly on her purchases . . . and her clutter.

A "You've Got Clutter" Quiz

Ask yourself, do I keep bringing more clutter into my life by:

A. Saying yes to everything everybody ever offers to give me?
B. Keeping every gift anyone has ever given me because I believe that's how you show love and feel loved?
C. Finding great bargains that I cannot pass up at garage, estate, and rummage sales and flea markets?
D. Finding wonderful things that people throw away?

If you answered yes to any of these questions, you need to work on the second Deadly Sin: You insist on bringing home stuff you don't need.

The Parent Curator

You have kept mementos of your children from when they were little to when they graduated from school, and beyond. Yet isn't it true that a few beloved items can evoke memories just as well as a huge collection of your children's things? A few baby clothes and one or two pieces of their artwork will work as well as several outfits and boxes of their artwork.

What is the purpose of mementos if you never look at them? Don't confuse clutter with memories. Your memories are in your heart, and you don't need to keep mementos from each stage of your child's childhood to cherish those memories. Separate the memory from the object.

Why Is It Hard to Let Go of Stuff?

Whether you have bought, found, collected, or been given your clutter doesn't matter. You now have a pretty good grasp of how clutter comes to live with you. Let's move on to some solutions, starting with a change in thought patterns.

You may say you hang on to clutter because you cherish your belongings. That may be true of a portion of your clutter, but the real reason is that you simply cannot throw it away. Let's explore some thoughts that might help you let go of some of it.

If you were poor as a child, saving rubber bands, boxes, and every chipped cookie jar you've ever owned may give you a sense of security. But if hard times hit, if you lose your job, you're not likely to support your family with eight thousand rubber bands and seven broken cookie jars.

Is your reason for keeping clutter because somebody might need it someday? Let's be honest; how often has a needy friend asked you for a broken cookie jar?

Are you keeping stuff you really don't like, use, need, or want because it *might* be valuable someday? Bear in mind that many people kept comic books, baseball cards, and Beanie Babies for years, only to find that when they tried to sell their "valuables," the buyers were willing to pay not much more than the purchase price. The time and space provided to these items over the years never paid off.

For some people, the accumulation of all that stuff is caused by a fear of scarcity or deprivation. They buy and stock up on food or other things that they consider to be necessities because they tell themselves, "I might need this someday." The accrued items give them an odd sense of security. If you sincerely need a sense of security, try this: Develop the habit of saving small amounts of money on a regular basis. Over time it really will add up to big bucks, and that is much better security than those seventeen cases of paper towels and 159 cans of dog food you've been saving (especially if you haven't had a dog for the past three years).

EXTRA CREDIT

1. Prepare yourself to de-clutter by doing these mental exercises this week.
   A. To help you get rid of some of your prized possessions, imagine:
      - Throwing out any of your possessions that are stained, broken, damaged beyond repair, or that nobody would ever want.
      - Selling, donating, or giving to someone all those things you don't need that are too good to toss out and that somebody else might want.
      - Saying good-bye to things that once brought joy and happy memories but now are in a dusty jumble of clutter.
   B. To stop bringing more clutter into your life, imagine:
      - Saying no to whoever is giving you things to bring home.

- Walking past a "prize" that someone put out with the trash, and leaving it where it is.
- Picking up something at a store, admiring it, and putting it back.

The more you practice these steps mentally, the easier it will be to eliminate some of your precious possessions and to resist the impulse to bring home more clutter.

2. Look at your work space and living space as if you are an outsider.
   Has clutter accumulated in places, but you were too "clutter numb" to notice? What areas startle you? Write them down.

   _____

   _____

   _____

   _____

3. Select one of those areas to work on. Every day (or every chance you get), "process" five items from that wild clutter.
   - Does the item have a happy home to live in? If so, put it there.
   - Does it *not* have a happy home? Assign one for it.
   - If, as you assess this area, you come across several items that you don't want to keep, get rid of them *now*.

4. Do you think your clutter accumulates because you:
   A. Save everything (whether you need it or want it or not)?
   B. Insist on bringing home (or allowing into your home) stuff you don't need?
   C. Never assign a place where each thing belongs?
   D. Set items aside until you "decide" about them?
   E. All of the above.

The insight gained here might help you know what to focus on. If your answer is "all of the above," don't let it discourage you. That's true for many of us.

5. Try out your new "Cultivate a Simple Habit" tip: If it takes less than one minute, do it now.

2

Gonna Take a Sentimental Journey

Not what we have, but what we enjoy,
constitutes our abundance.
—*John Petit-Senn*, poet

Letting go of mementos, photos, collections, or gifts you've become sentimentally and emotionally attached to can be very difficult. At no time is that more true than when a loved one dies. You may need months or years to go by before you are able to decide what to keep and what to get rid of.

When my mother died, we didn't have the luxury of allowing much time to pass. She lived in a different state, and her home had to be emptied so it could be sold. Otherwise we would have incurred huge expenses, including the mortgage, taxes, utilities, and home insurance. Also, we didn't want to risk any damage that weather or vandals might do to an unoccupied house.

When we flew to Florida to clear out her place, I brought my teenage daughter Kerry with me. As we sorted through Mom's treasures, we laughed and cried, sharing favorite memories. It would have been torture for me to do this alone. For such emotionally draining work, you need someone to be with you. I was lucky to have had someone I loved with me, but even a stranger can be helpful with this difficult task. If you don't know anyone who can help, call a local church or other house of worship and explain that you need someone with you as you go through your loved one's things. The staff will understand and find someone to help you.

Together, Kerry and I decided to get rid of what was junk and what we wanted to keep. Then we set up everything else on display and invited Mom's friends and neighbors to come over and select items to remember her by or to help themselves to anything they could use or somebody they knew could use.

We planned to donate anything left over to a worthy cause; then a friend of Mom's offered to do that work for us by delivering everything to Mom's favorite charity. We hoped that most of her stuff would be appreciated and maybe even cherished. It was that hope that helped me let go of so much.

That hope . . . plus Kerry. She would question every single thing I wanted to keep. "Do you really want to pay to ship that home? Do you want to have it take up space when you know we don't have a place to put it? Will you ever, ever use it? What will you do—hide it in a crawl space and pretend that it brings back memories for you? You'll pack it away, and when you die, I'll have to get rid of it."

Kerry was very persuasive. She made sense. And so, a few short weeks after my mother died, we got rid of most of her stuff. We kept a few items: her Bible, a few things to hang on the wall, some porcelain figures, serving pieces, special holiday ornaments (but not the whole box), and the angel tree topper.

None of the young newly married relatives wanted the china that Grandma had served her holiday meals on, and Kerry didn't want it either. So we gave it away and never once regretted it. Our memories of holidays with her are beautiful; her china was ugly.

We have not regretted any of the other things we eliminated. In fact, we don't even remember what we got rid of that week. But none of us forget Mom. You don't need a heap of clutter to bring back happy memories of those you love.

GETTING READY TO GET RID OF IT

By this point, you probably are ready to say good-bye to some of your clutter. You realize you can't move forward until you discard whatever you don't really need or want. Long ago you probably acknowledged that you have too much stuff.

I promise never to ask you to throw away your treasures. If you were asked to simply toss out your clutter, some of you might do it. But in the middle of the night, while the rest of the world dozes, you just might tiptoe out to the trash bin, drag every bit of discarded clutter back into the house, and, if the trash has already been collected, wander around mumbling "Woe is me! How I miss my box of buttons."

Therefore, I don't expect you to toss your beloved stuff into the trash. Things you absolutely love you should keep—unless you don't have room for them all. The objective of this book is to help you conquer clutter that is causing you stress and taking up space you don't have. If you love giving your time, space, care, and energy to these mementos, and it's not causing problems for anyone, then leave them be.

However, if you wish you had more space with less clutter, confusion, and chaos, consider this: Those mementos that are "on display" may once have been cherished reminders of happy times, but now that plastic statue of Mount Rushmore and that coffee mug from Disneyland have likely transformed into clutter.

In addition, all those mementos *not* on display, and which you never look at because they are packed away someplace, are not providing happy memories for you.

How much are you keeping not because you want to but because you think you should keep it or that it's wrong to get rid of it?

The best way that you can say good-bye to an item you feel an emotional attachment to is to pass it on to some place or person that will value it and appreciate it and prize it as much as you do.

HANDING DOWN BABY FURNITURE

A neighbor's offhand comment led Ingrid to view hand-me-downs in a whole new light, take action, and gain much-needed space.

"My neighbor noticed a corner of my garage was filled with big boxes of baby buggies, strollers, cribs, and other baby furniture," Ingrid explained. "When she asked, I told her I was holding on to them to hand down to the next generation.

"My neighbor said, 'You know, hand-it-down doesn't mean you *have* to hand it down to your kids. You could hand it down now to someone who needs it.'"

"Those words rocked my world," Ingrid continued. "What my neighbor didn't know was I also was saving almost all the books and toys my children ever had—also to hand down. I immediately realized that I could easily give away these things; my kids wouldn't care one bit, and I even knew who I'd offer them to first.

"I had met a woman on my block who was expecting a baby, and her husband had just been laid off work. I went and asked her if she'd like the baby furniture, and with tears in her eyes she told me I was the answer to her prayers. Neither of them had any relatives in this country, and they didn't want to worry their family by letting them know that the husband was out of work. But they were starting to feel desperate. And then I showed up.

"Since then I've given everything away (except for a few small, special items for each of my children), and it was all so deeply appreciated that I felt wonderful. Besides, getting rid of all those boxes means the second car can actually fit in the garage."

A "You've Got Clutter" Quiz

Do you collect and refuse to throw out mementos because:

A. You have an emotional attachment to your bridesmaid dress from twenty-one years ago or the warranty for your eight-track tape player that broke a lifetime ago?

B. You really want to read the kindergarten newsletter of your youngest son (who just graduated from college), or your notes from college, high school, scout troop meetings, and every seminar you've ever attended?

C. You fear that your personal history will disappear if you do not save T-shirts, ticket stubs, and programs of every event you've ever attended?

D. You're afraid that all your happy memories will evaporate if you do not save every souvenir from every place you've ever visited or every trip you've ever taken?

E. You think hanging on to old stuff means you can hang on to your youth or some former (happier?) version of yourself or people you love?

If you answered yes to any of the above, you are emotional about getting rid of anything. You are not alone, and this book will help you select what to keep and to find a place where you can give away the rest.

MEMORIES

We're not trying to get rid of memories. We're trying to downsize the overwhelming mementos to the point where you can enjoy them. Clutter really gets in the way of your happy memories.

- Keep the memento if it gives you joy and delight; get rid of it if it does not and you don't have a *real* reason to keep it.

- Ask yourself: Maybe this item brought joy to me once, but does it still bring joy as I dust it or look for places to put it or feel overwhelmed by having it and so many other things taking up space in my home? Do I really want to be a caretaker of this item?
- If your household includes children, give each one a "Memory Box" to hold souvenirs and to keep in their rooms. If it starts to overflow, they will learn the important lesson of putting boundaries on "stuff" and eliminating something.
- If your kids have grown up and moved out, gather all of the things you are saving from your childhood or theirs. Make a box for each family member and put appropriate items in each box. Include bronze shoes, clay hand molds, handmade valentines, letters, toys, locks of hair, baby books, photos, and anything else you are saving. Invite them over and make a big deal of giving the precious items to them for safekeeping.

- Gather up other sentimental items you've saved yet have no use for. Let the kids select and divide what they want. Then sell, donate, or toss in the trash everything they don't want. That's what the kids would do if you died tomorrow.
- You can honor the memory of a loved one by donating his or her cookware, encyclopedia, toys, books, or sports equipment to a worthy cause, where it will be valued and used.
- Your dad's record collection or your mom's saltshaker collection meant a lot to them, but if you get rid of these mementos, that does not mean you don't love them.
- Find ways to display items you want to keep because they are special. Shadow box frames can display many items at once. Make "theme" displays for trip souvenirs, special occasions, or of school years.

TOO TRUE TO ARGUE

Getting rid of mementos of someone you love does not mean that you no longer love that person or vice versa.
Getting rid of a gift given to you does not mean that you no longer love the gift giver.
Getting rid of belongings of people who have passed away does not mean that you no longer love them or that you will forget them.

When a Collection Becomes Clutter

Collections are a wonderful source of comfort and enjoyment. They only become clutter when they are through serving their purpose, you no longer enjoy them, and they are taking up valuable room needed for other purposes.

In that case, it's time to make some decisions about this collection. You decide:

1. to stop adding to the collection and
2. what to do with the items you have collected.

You can break the collecting habit in a number of ways. For some, it is a simple matter to stop buying or bringing home model aircraft carriers or eighteenth-century candle snuffers. But that doesn't work for everyone.

Sophia had collected dolls for years. They filled a glass case, four shelves, and a china cabinet, took over the room and eventually the house. One day, Sophia decided it wasn't reasonable to find new spots in the house for her dolls because no matter where she put them, they became dust collectors and created a cluttered, junky look.

When you don't have room for all your stuff, you don't need more room, you need less stuff.

The collection had provided happiness and pleasure to Sophia for a long time, but now she realized that her house did not have unlimited space to accommodate her little friends and she finally accepted the fact that some of them had to go. It was time for her dolls to "retire," and Sophia made the difficult decision to stop buying them.

Very soon she regretted her decision. Sophia's work took her all over the world, and during her travels she had loved searching for and finding new dolls. She sincerely missed the thrill of the hunt and now realized that once the dolls were home, and she had showed them to her friends and placed them in a spot with the others, she didn't pay much attention to them.

Her decision to stop buying was a mistake. Sophia, like many other collectors, delighted in finding a rare bargain or filling in a gap in her collection or stumbling across a unique beauty much more than she enjoyed actually owning the items. So she hit upon a new plan.

She selected a group of dolls that she would keep forever, and carefully arranged them in the glass display case. Then she counted up over 450 dolls that she would not mind parting with. Every few months, she packed up 20 to 30 of these dolls and delivered them to a nearby hospital. Eventually, the nurse who grew to know Sophia invited her to join in traveling from one little girl's room to another delivering dolls.

Today Sophia is "The Doll Lady" who appears at hospitals and homeless shelters giving gorgeous dolls from around the world to brighten the day of little girls.

She still has the joy of searching for and purchasing beautiful dolls from all over, enjoying them as long as she wants before giving them away. She now also is a collector of smiles and hugs from sweet little girls.

The Magnificent Obsessions of Collections

A participant in one of my seminars had a sign in his home that read, *There is a fine line between collections and mental illness.* We all laughed when he told us about it, but many people admit to a certain obsessiveness about their collections. Some say that eventually they have a collection of collections. They must learn when to say "Enough!" Learning that lesson makes a collection manageable, and the collector can enjoy each piece, instead of being overwhelmed by it all.

Anne Morrow Lindbergh addresses this subject in her book *Gift from the Sea:* "To ask how little, not how much, can I get along with. To say—is it necessary?—when I am tempted to add one more accumulation to my life. . . . One cannot collect all the beautiful shells on the beach. One can collect only a few, and they are more beautiful if they are few."*

If you cannot stop the collectibles from coming in, can't part with them, and you're running out of space, here are some tips:

- Pack the entire collection away with hopes of enjoying it again at another time.
- Put it in the attic, basement, garage, or some other safe place.
- Find a manageable way to display it that will not collect dust or be knocked over by the cats or take up valuable space that you could use for something else.

*A Gift from the Sea, New York: Pantheon Books, 1955, 35 and 114.

- A bookcase or shelves hung on the wall or a cabinet with glass doors can display many collections.
- A net in the upper corner of a child's room can hold stuffed animals. Once the child has a place to put his collection and can see all of it, invite him to select his favorite ones, and give away the others.
- A cardboard box, along with some plastic sleeves, helps you organize a collection of magazines or comic books. You can file each precious book publication by date or other category.
- Do not build a shed for your collection or—worse—do not pay your hard-earned cash for a storage place to house your collection. When you have to pay to store it, it is time to regain control of your collection.

- When you see your collections on display, it may be easier for you to weed out the junky stuff and keep the best of the best.
- Announce to the world—well, at least to your family and others who give you gifts—that you no longer collect whatever it is that is overwhelming you and overtaking your home. You might disappoint people who loved the challenge of buying you wombat figurines or whatever it is you collected, so be prepared to give them another suggestion if they ask. Otherwise they just might decide to start you on another collection, and suddenly your home is overflowing with pink flamingos.

If you are saving a collectible as an investment, do some research into its value or potential value. You might discover that you are putting hundreds of dollars' worth of time and effort into taking care of items that fifty years from now will bring you $17.43 if you are lucky.

If you plan to leave your collection to your adult children, have a heart-to-heart talk with them *now* to see if they would want these items. If not, realize that your cherished items might be more burden than bounty to your heirs.

LET THEM KNOW WHAT IS VALUABLE

Do you keep your valuable possessions and collections in dust-covered boxes amid clutter? If so, people coming across these boxes after your death are apt to toss them because they don't know how valuable their contents are.

In the case of George's aunt Nora, it wasn't death but a move to a nursing home that prompted her family to clear out her house. Nora's idea of leading a frugal life was to never throw away anything, so it was exhausting work emptying the house. The contents of the basement alone filled a Dumpster twice.

Soon after Nora's move to the nursing home, George attended a family holiday gathering at which his niece made a disturbing announcement. "You know how we all thought Nora was poor as a church mouse?" she said. "Well, I just found out some of those boxes of glass that we gave away and threw in the trash contained extremely expensive Waterford crystal that she inherited from her mother."

Gifts—It's the Thought That Counts

Do you have every single gift you've received since your first birthday? You may not know who gave you a particular item or even what it is, but you keep it because . . . it's a gift.

Do you hold on to a gift as if the giver intended that you would make a lifetime commitment to it? Surely you don't expect that of others when you give them a gift—why would they expect it of you?

Give away or toss gifts you no longer want. The givers probably won't notice. If they *do* notice (and certain people in your life just might do that), you can say:

- "I loved it, but it broke."
- "I can't find it."
- "It wore out, so I had to get rid of it."
- "A poor family really needed it, so I gave it to them." (Your best friend asks, "A poor family really needed a black velour sequined Elvis pillow from Las Vegas?" You answer, "Yep.")
- Or to prevent future gift-giving challenges, you could tell the truth: "I really appreciate the thought and money

that you put into my gift, but I'm working very hard at simplifying my life and have been giving away many of my possessions to people needier than I am. For future gifts, can I suggest . . ."

SUGGESTIONS FOR NONCLUTTER GIFTS

Good communication is the key to getting the gifts you want. When gift givers ask you what you'd like for an occasion, *tell them*. If they don't ask, let them know that you'd be glad to offer some suggestions. Be specific. Give them a description of the item you want and tell them what store you've seen it in. Or pick several items in a range of prices from a catalog, so givers will have a choice, and you will receive something you'll really like.

If you don't want more stuff and you know that people absolutely, positively *have* to buy you something, give them helpful ideas. Tell them you are cutting down on *things* in your life and would prefer, for example:

- a gift certificate to a restaurant or for a massage at a spa
- a membership to a museum, zoo, or some cultural organization
- a commitment to spend a day or an afternoon together
- two hours of help clutter-busting your closets
- tickets to a movie or play
- a contribution to your favorite charity
- a book you can read and then give to a friend or the library

Don't let yourself become miserable because well-meaning people who love you keep giving you things you neither need nor want. To become a gracious recipient *and* a person who has clutter under control, you have to communicate creatively and gently with the people who care enough to offer their gifts.

What if a gift giver doesn't get it or doesn't know about your new efforts to de-clutter, and a gift that you don't need and will never use slips under the radar? Here's what Mike has to say on this subject: "Sometimes you're just stuck with gifts and have to hold on to them for a while before you can get rid of them. If you are extremely close to the gift giver, you might explain that you can't use the gift. But most of us would rather endure do-it-yourself root canal than go through that because you risk hurting someone you love. So we let some time go by and then secretly, quietly, like a thief in the night, we let it slip out of our lives.

"And then we redouble our efforts to prevent it from happening again by repeating—again—suggestions for gifts that won't turn into clutter."

LEAVE IT IN THE MUSEUM

Every time Otto admired something in a store, his well-meaning wife would ask him if she could buy it for him. He'd say no, and then she'd sneak back and buy it to surprise him "because he loved it."

Upon receiving the gift he didn't want, he never said anything because he didn't want to hurt his wife's feelings. Then one day shortly before they both left town on vacation, during which she was certain to buy some more unwanted gifts for him, he finally explained to her that when he admires something in a store, to him it's as if he were admiring something in a museum.

He might love it. Its beauty might give him goose bumps. But in a museum, you keep walking and leave it for others also to enjoy. That's how he feels when he points out something beautiful in a store. He doesn't need or want to accumulate more stuff in his life, even though he enjoys admiring beautiful things. If his wife wants to buy a particular item for herself, fine. But he is not hinting that he wants it; he's just admiring it.

So now when he comments on an item, his wife says, "I know, I know, let's leave it in the museum . . . I mean store . . . for others to enjoy."

TOO MANY PARTY GIFTS

When you're having a party that is a gift-giving occasion, you can either say nothing and receive a load of stuff you don't need or want—*or* be a risk taker and suggest that guests bring something to the party other than gifts. For example, your invitation might include the line: "No gifts, but if you *can't* come empty-handed, please bring food, which we'll deliver to our local food pantry." I know of one wedding where the guests brought more than six hundred pounds of canned goods for the homeless.

If it's a traditional family party, you can suggest that guests bring gifts for children only, or have a grab bag where each person buys for just one other person. Some parents have become creative problem solvers about their children's cluttered lives (and rooms!), and have curtailed the number of gifts at birthday parties. One family sent invitations to their daughter's birthday party that instructed the guests to bring, in lieu of gifts, various items to work on a craft project (beads, feathers, paints, brushes). The birthday girl's big brothers contributed shirts they were ready to throw out. Each child pulled a "paint shirt" over his or her clothes, and instead of games, they all painted little birdhouses. That was their take-home gift. All the kids remember the party, and nobody complained about not receiving a goodie bag.

Another birthday invitation requested that each guest bring a toy not for the birthday boy but for a child in a homeless shelter. At this party, instead of games, the children all got into the host family's van and helped deliver the toys.

I can see you rolling your eyes. You cannot imagine any child you know wanting this type of party. You're not alone; many people have the same reaction when they hear these suggestions. But consider the other option: the typical birthday party.

Guests bring toys and clothes that your child—let's say it's your son—doesn't like or already has or doesn't need or appreciate because he has so many others. Afterward, your overwhelmed, overstimulated son has an attitude of "Is that all there is?" and you are at your wit's end because he has just too much stuff and no place to put it. So the room is messy and cluttered, and your son has no sense of appreciation or joy because *he has so much that he values nothing.*

It's time to stop thinking that we don't have any control over incoming clutter caused by getting so many gifts. Once you make up your mind, you can gain control over gift giving without hurting anyone's feelings.

ORGANIZING PHOTOS

First, gather all your photos into one box, basket, or corner of a room. Start watching for sales on photo albums.

Next, divide the photos into manageable categories such as:

- person
- year
- pets
- vacations
- holidays

Put the categorized pictures into shoe boxes, folders, envelopes, or baskets. Be sure to label them. Then, while you're watching TV or listening to the radio, go through one category at a time.

Keep only the great pictures. Be ruthless in tossing out bad, fuzzy, and unflattering photos.

Brooke selects only the very best photos for herself and passes along other perfectly good photos to her daughter as well as her nieces and nephews. (She gave them all photo albums to keep these pictures.)

Sometimes she even has enough extra photos to mail to a few friends and relatives who would enjoy seeing them.

Once you have winnowed down the photos, take one category at a time and put the pictures in albums.

From this day forward, date your photos as soon as you get them, and sort through, keeping only the best ones, then place them in an envelope until you are ready to put them in an album or whatever photo-storage system you prefer.

Photos should be stored in a cool, dry place. Don't keep them in an attic, basement, or garage. The best rule of thumb: Store pictures in the same environment in which you would feel most comfortable.

PHOTO IDEAS THAT CUT DOWN ON CLUTTER

Take pictures of:

- Items with sentimental value that you need to dispose of. Instead of a room full of stuff, you'll have an album full.
- The kids' art and science projects. Give them copies to keep in their photo albums.

No matter what items you may have a sentimental attachment to—souvenirs from trips, collections of dolls or trains, photographs, or gifts—you'll have an easier time parting with them once they've turned into clutter if you've *already* determined the best ways (for you) to dispose of them. Then your struggle to let go of an item will be offset by the knowledge that some person or organization would be delighted to receive it and put it to good use—or just enjoy having it. The suggestions in the next chapter will help you decide what to do with your stuff.

EXTRA CREDIT

1. Evaluate your collection(s).
   - Does it still bring you joy?
   - Do you need to find a creative way to display it?
   - Do you need to set boundaries on it?
   - Could you get rid of the items you no longer love and cherish?

2. If you want to stop incoming gifts or collectibles, practice telling one friend or relative that you no longer collect whatever is overwhelming you. You don't have to tell the whole world; practice with just one person.

3. If you suspect that someone will give you a gift this year, practice how you will tell that person what you'd like.

Part II

❦❖❦

Get Rid of Clutter
and Keep It Out

3
Fifty Ways to Leave
Your Clutter

Letting go of a material possession is an important action. It makes room for "something else," which might be energy or serenity or joy or clarity or a nicer, newer, better version of what you've let go of. The following anecdote, which I call "The Circle of Couch Giving," illustrates this point beautifully.

When Danielle and her husband, Alec, were moving out of one house, they were concerned about transporting a big, heavy over-sized sleeper sofa to their new house where it probably would not fit in anyway. The fellow moving into their old house offered to buy it, but Danielle and Alec created a win-win situation by giving it to him.

A few weeks after the couple moved into the new house, a friend of Danielle's bought a new couch and gave them her old small one, which fit perfectly. Then, when their son was born, they needed to put a crib in the room where the small couch was, so they passed the couch on to a friend who needed a new one. In each instance, everyone was happy, and the circle of giving worked perfectly.

Never be afraid to give away material possessions. Amazing things happen when you do. (Alec swears that every time he gives away an unneeded tool to someone, a tool that he does need miraculously comes into his life.) This chapter is chock-full of ways to "leave your clutter."

TAKE TIME TO DECIDE, CLYDE

The first step in leaving behind your clutter, before you even touch one thing, is to:

1. Decide where your stuff is going, whether you want to sell it or donate it; then figure out how and where you will do that.

WAYS YOU CAN SELL, NELL

2. Place a classified ad.
3. Put up flyers on local bulletin boards such as those in grocery stores.
4. Run a garage sale on your own, or with several friends, or with the whole block (as many houses as possible).

Garage sales can be hard work and time consuming, and they are not for cowards. It can be painful to watch people rummage through your stuff and then walk away because they don't want it. If it's not for you, don't do it. (Marketing tip: Instead of tagging and pricing every item, just put up a sign, *Make Me a Reasonable Offer I Won't Refuse*. And rather than using the typical garage sale sign, you might try: *Come On Over. Our Beautiful Trash Could Become Your Beautiful Treasure*. Or *Buyers Beware! Bargains Galore!*

5. Sell at an estate sale, flea market, or rummage sale.

6. Tell friends, neighbors, family, or coworkers about what is for sale. Let them stop by whenever they like.

BE A TECHNO-GEEK, DEKE

7. Sell on eBay.com.

8. If you belong to a computer group, post a notice on the list-serve about what you want to sell or give away.

9. Sell on auctions.yahoo.com.

10. Try freecycle.org, an organization that has message boards where people in your locale can post what they are giving away or what they are looking for. All for free.

11. Post on an e-mail list of a local group. It is amazing what people will come and haul away.

12. Find a place to pass on your old computer and other high-tech goodies. Even though you paid big bucks for them, when they become useless, it doesn't make sense to

hang on to them. They aren't going to have a miraculous healing or rise from the dead. Call the people who service your computer and ask for information about charities or recycling centers that can use, recycle, or refurbish old computers and other techie toys.

HOW ABOUT A TRADE, WADE

13. Create an exchange—magazines, books, coupons, whatever. Take a box to work and start a swap by placing a sign on the box inviting others to contribute and to help themselves.

14. Have a "trade party." For example, extend invitations to your friends who wear about the same size and styles as you. Have them come to your home with clothes they want to give away. Then put out the clothes and let everyone swap. Or have a poker night for those CDs you haven't played in decades. ("I'll see your Rod Stewart and raise you one Duran Duran".) Donate the leftovers to the library or any organization that collects used items for fund-raisers such as rummage sales.

CHOOSE TO DONATE, KATE

15. Find a worthy cause and donate to it. You won't make any money, but you might get a receipt to use as a tax deduction. Always call first before delivering your donation. And bear in mind that some charities will accept or even

Some places and organizations that would love your donations:

- Salvation Army
- Goodwill Industries
- Synagogues, churches, and St. Vincent DePaul Society
- Thrift shops that raise funds for worthy causes
- Foster homes
- Shelters for the homeless or for battered women
- Animal shelters (old towels and linens for animal bedding or cleaning up)
- Hospitals (magazines, gently used toys or clothes, especially sweats for patients in the ER who've had their clothes cut off or ruined)
- Doctors' offices (magazines, ballpoint pens, toys for a "kiddie korner")
- Nursing homes (craft supplies, plants, magazines, blankets or afghans, anything that might brighten up the day of someone who never has visitors; consider delivering the items yourself and visiting with a lonely soul)
- Schools (art or office supplies, materials for decorations or class projects, supplies for sewing classes)
- Libraries (books for public libraries, especially at "Friends of the Library" fund-raisers, and for school libraries)
- Veterans' groups (see "They'll Come to You, Lou")
- Theater groups (furniture, wall hangings, clothes, jewelry)
- Any organization fund-raiser holding a "silent auction" (unused items in their original packaging)
- Quilting guilds (fabric and needlework supplies)

pick up large items like old cars, office equipment, and furniture.

THEY'LL COME TO YOU, LOU

16. Call Disabled Veterans, Vietnam Veterans, Purple Heart Veterans, or Amvets to come and pick up your donations. Some veterans' groups and other charities will even put your name on their calling list and phone you every six weeks or so, when their truck will be in your neighborhood. All you have to do is put your bags or boxes of stuff outside, and they will pick them up.

DISPOSE WHERE IT'S SAFE, RAPHE

17. Contact your town clerk or sanitation department to check where you can safely dispose of environmentally hazardous materials such as old batteries, motor oil, paints, insecticides, aerosol spray cans, and so forth.

CALL PEOPLE WHO KNOW, BEAU

18. Call those folks who know about worthy causes in your area, such as: librarians, village or town clerks, clergy, community leaders, aldermen and -women, and staff members at family service centers.

HELP THOSE IN NEED, REED

19. Set up in your home (or at work) a big plastic bag or a box. Place this donation container in a closet, pantry, corner of the garage, or office. That way, anytime anyone makes the decision to get rid of something, he or she can put it in the donation container. (Or the contents of the container can be earmarked for your next garage sale.)

20. Use creativity when you give to others. (Misha delivered to a battered women's shelter six old suitcases, each with a stuffed animal inside. Although the suitcases were "un-trendy," they were better than the plastic bags in which many of the women carried their belongings. And the stuffed animals brought pleasure to the women's children or, if they had none, to the women themselves.)

JUST GIVE IT AWAY, RAY

When you give an item to a private party, you won't get a tax deduction, but you'll have the satisfaction of helping someone and expecting nothing in return.

21. Give it away to someone you know who needs it: a family member, a friend, a coworker, a neighbor.

22. Put the items on your front lawn with a big sign: *Free.* (One person's junk truly *is* another person's treasure.) You can also do this after a yard sale; rather than cart the unsold items back inside, everything goes to the curb with the sign *Free* on it. Whatever no one takes can stay there for the trash collector.

DONATE A TOOL, JEWEL

For duplicate tools or ones you'll never use:

23. Pass them on to newlyweds.

24. Give them to anyone moving into a first house or apartment or who is recently divorced.

25. Donate them to a high school vocational class.

26. Give them to a local theater group.

27. Donate them to a church or food pantry connected with people who are starting over.

28. Contribute them to Habitat for Humanity.

DON'T SEND STUFF THAT'S ICKY, MICKEY

29. Send just the good stuff. The poor deserve dignity. Homeless and needy persons have had enough hard times. Don't make it harder by donating items that are stained, broken, damaged beyond repair, or that nobody would ever want.

IT'S TIME TO TOSS, ROSS

As much as you hate to throw things away, you may have to. Nobody really wants that dented coffee can full of rusty nuts and bolts, or those broken toasters. Of course, you might plan on fixing the toaster. Ahem. When it was time to fix it, did you? If you didn't fix it *then*, will you fix it *now?* If not, admit that it's time to send it to toaster heaven.

30. Throw the item in the trash.
31. Rent a Dumpster and shovel the stuff into it.
32. Take it to a garbage dump. (My friend Sheila, who just turned seventy, sent me the following message about the joys of garbage dumps: "I have discovered a new favorite pastime—dump runs. Nothing quite matches the exhilaration of standing in the back of a pickup, lined in a row with all the construction trucks, and heaving boxes of assorted debris into the waiting, crunching jaws of a giant bulldozer. Ah, Rita, it doesn't get any better than that!")

MAKE A FAMILY CALL, PAUL

When you have family heirlooms or photos that are just collecting dust (you don't really want them but can't throw them out):

33. Contact members of your immediate family (such as your siblings and your adult children); tell them you don't want these items, and ask if anyone wants them.

34. If they don't want them, call or write to cousins, nieces, nephews, and other relatives.

35. If there still are no takers, look around for others— family friends or those with the same last name or nationality—and offer the items to them. They might cherish what your family doesn't want.

GET RID OF THOSE CLOTHES, ROSE

36. Find a charity that means a lot to you. Then it can be a genuine joy to pass on your clothes. (As a pharmaceutical saleswoman, Marge has a large wardrobe of business clothes. She has developed a special relationship with an organization that collects business attire for low-income women entering the workplace. When Marge cleans out her closet, she puts each outfit she no longer wants, along with the matching shoes and accessories, in a box and donates it to this organization. It warms her heart each time she hears about a woman who felt and looked terrific in one of her donated outfits—and ultimately landed a job.)

> ## CULTIVATE A SIMPLE HABIT
> When you find someone
> Who loves your stuff,
> To give it up
> Won't be so tough.

37. Sell your clothes at a secondhand store.

38. Deliver them to a nursing home.

39. Give them to your favorite charity for an upcoming rummage sale.

40. Find a family with children younger than yours. Offer to regularly give them hand-me-downs. Don't ask for the clothes to be returned.

THAT COULD BE ART, BART

41. Make keepsake albums for kids with a three-ring binder. Include pictures, certificates, cards or letters, and add your own comments. Children can keep the albums in their rooms and will come to treasure the memories you are providing.

42. Gather up anything that has craft-project potential, including magazines, empty thread spools, buttons, pictures, and small plastic thingamajigs, and donate it to a scout troop or a teacher (of art classes, preschool, elementary grades, or Sunday school).

WRITE DOWN A DATE, NATE

43. Take items you haven't used in the past year and put them in a box. Mark the box with a date that's six months or a year from now. When the time is up, toss out the box, donate it, or get rid of it some other way. Do not look inside. You haven't used these items or even missed them, so let them go.

SHARE THAT MAGAZINE, DEAN

Cross out or tear off your address label from old magazines or even catalogs. Then:

44. Pass them on to a child-care center, for use in crafts projects.

45. Leave them in doctors', dentists', and hospital waiting rooms.

46. Give them to beauty salons.

47. Set them out at the lunch area at your office.

48. Donate them to a senior center or nursing home.

49. Give them to libraries to sell at fund-raising events.

ASK SOMEONE YOU KNOW, JOE

50. Ask a friend to take away the stuff that you don't need but can't throw out. Let your friend decide what to do with it. (As I started to convert from my Pack Rat life, I asked my clutter-hating friend, Dorothy, to help me dispose of things that I found hard to throw away. No matter what I had,

Dorothy would say, "I know a poor family that can use that." Then she'd cart away my useless stuff. I knew she headed straight for the trash can and dumped everything, but that was fine with me because I could not throw it away myself.)

There are many more ways than these fifty to find people and places who would love to receive your stuff. Be creative, look around, and ask around to see where you want your clutter to end up. That will make it easier and more comfortable to let go.

The important thing to remember is that before you even start to tackle that stack of clutter, decide who will be the happy recipient of your stuff. Otherwise, you won't be able to say good-bye to many items that you don't need or use.

EXTRA CREDIT

1. Decide what you'll do with your nonkeepers.

2. Do your homework before selling or donating items. Will you be having a garage sale? Set a date, recruit helpers, get signs, and find out if you need approval from your city or village. Did you decide to donate? Select an organization, find its phone number, check out what items it will accept, as well as how, when, and where you should deliver them.

3. Also, decide on a permanent place to put your "donation/garage sale" bags or boxes so that when anyone in your home wants to pass on something, he or she will know where to put it.

4. Put the bags or boxes there right now.

4

How to Start?
Work It Smart

Waiting until everything is perfect before
making a move is like waiting to start a trip
until all the traffic lights are green.
—Karen Ireland, *author of*
The Job Survival Instruction Book

You have taken the first step and decided how you will dispose of those items you don't need or want. You also have a plan for where and how you'll sell or donate this stuff. Now it's finally time to attack that clutter. Don't put it off with an excuse like "I'll tackle that clutter when I have a whole day free." Or "I'll sort through all that when this busy time ends." You'll never have a whole free day, will you? And do you really believe that busy time will *ever* end? No matter how busy you are, you can always find a free hour. Maybe not an hour a day, but an hour here or there, at least an hour a week.

Take the STING Out of De-Cluttering

Select just one small area to de-clutter.

Not the whole kitchen, just the one counter. Not the whole garage, just one shelf or one corner. If there is a huge mound of stuff, just attack one type of thing first (let's say paper), then put away another type (tools). Take it one step at a time.

Time it. Give that clutter one full hour.

Set a timer for sixty minutes. The tick-tick-ticking creates a sense of urgency. One reason to stop after an hour is that much of de-cluttering is making decisions, and after one hour, you'll be so exhausted that you'll need a break.

Ignore everything else.

In Shirley's case, it was the "everything else" that *always* got her into trouble. When planning to clean the garage, for example, she would head out toward it, focused on her target. But on the way, she'd stop to wipe off the counter and load the dishwasher. And even before she finished these tasks she'd begin sorting through the mail; then she had to check on one of the bills and call a friend about the invitation to a cook-out that just arrived in the mail. As the sun was setting, she'd have numerous jobs started but none completed. She would shrug and say, "Well, I was multitasking."

Similarly, when she started to attack the clutter on her desk, she'd soon lose her focus. She'd decide to just spend one minute checking her e-mails, then make three quick phone

calls, then play one—just one—computer game. And in the blink of an eye, she'd look at the clock and decide that it was too late to tackle that clutter, so she'd do it tomorrow . . . maybe.

Learn from Shirley's mistakes. Follow this rule: While that timer is ticking, ignore everything else.

No breaks before the bell rings.
By following this and the previous rule, you will do one hour of pure work and will be amazed at what you can accomplish. That means if you come across a box of bell-bottoms and beads from the sixties or your class essays from high school— as long as that timer is ticking—do *not* stop to stroll down memory lane.

Give yourself a reward.
A trip to Hawaii would be a great prize for cleaning out your junk drawer, but it's not gonna happen. What can you give yourself? If you're stumped, here are some ideas.

- Promise yourself that after you've put in an hour on de-cluttering you can have your favorite drink or watch a TV show you enjoy.
- Oddly enough, many of us put off doing things we enjoy— spending time with friends, reading novels or magazines, going to the movies or zoo, working out, playing the piano, walking in nature. After one hour of clutter-busting, wallow in one of your favorite leisure activities . . . guilt-free.

A word of caution: When you've just de-cluttered an area,
don't reward yourself by going out and buying stuff to bring in
and clutter it up again.

START SMART

By now, you might have recognized that a cluttered environment contributes to cluttered thinking, and cluttered thinking
contributes to procrastination. And procrastination is often
what started the clutter in the first place. The best way to break
that vicious circle is to START Smart:

Select ahead of time what you'll do with the nonkeepers (see chapter 3).

Tape labels on bags or boxes. Toss, deliver, put away, donate/sell.
Set up separate containers for items you will donate, recycle,
sell, and toss before you start de-cluttering. Otherwise, you'll
do the clutter shuffle—just moving stuff from one spot to another. By the way, make sure the *biggest* container is a wastebasket.

Also, set up bags or boxes for items you will keep and put away later. Containers for keepers and nonkeepers should be clearly labeled.

Attack the edges first.
In the office, first clear off the top of the file cabinet, the book-case, the windowsills, and the stacks on the floor. In the dining room, clear clutter off the floor and all the side tables before you start on the dining table. Every time you enter the office or dining room, you'll feel terrific at your success. Then, when you are finally ready to attack the big clutter on your desk or dining room table, you'll already have empty areas to stack and sort stuff.

Recruit a friend to help you make decisions.
Much of clutter-busting is deciding what to keep and where to keep it, and what to discard and where to discard it. A great deal of all this stuff has accumulated because you put off making decisions in the first place. If you still struggle with those decisions and find that to be the hardest part, it's time to recruit a helper.

Toss, recycle, or somehow get rid of most of it.
Make up your mind as you start clutter-busting that you will get rid of the majority of your clutter. If you can't decide about an item—if you're on the fence—get rid of it.

Toss your clutter if:

After hearing a keynote address presented at a conference, Brynn sent me an e-mail with her observations on recruiting friends:

Dear Rita,

You're right. When I asked my friends, I was amazed to hear that several are awesome at living free of clutter, and when you said they might be happy to help me, that was the understatement of the century. These women are thrilled to come over and help me get rid of my clutter.

My friend Jessica danced with joy when she came over to help me clear out my closet, and just kept shouting, "Toss, toss, toss, Hallelujah!"

Here's a warning to give people. Tell them BEWARE and do NOT invite a fellow Clutter Glutton (as you call them) to help de-clutter. My brain must have flown out the window when I invited my sister (who is just as much into clutter as I am) to come over to help me de-clutter the kitchen. She encouraged me to keep everything except a few scraps of paper and one melted plastic food-saver lid. Then we went out shopping. She sabotaged my plan, and she did it all so gleefully.

Now I'm back on track and back to de-cluttering. Like you've said, someday I might be able to do this all my myself, but for now, I'm calling on my clutter-busting friends.

- You had forgotten you have it.
- It's broken or obsolete.
- You haven't used it in months or years.
- It's the wrong size, color, or style.

- It takes up space, you have to clean it, even insure it, but you don't get much use or enjoyment from it.

Be honest with yourself. If you never saw the item again, you would never think of it. And if you don't love it now, why would you think you'll love it later?

THE FIRST TIME IS THE HARDEST

In getting started with tossing out clutter, the first time is the hardest. Although de-cluttering eventually will leave you feeling lighter, happier, and freer, parting with some items may cause anxiety. Sometimes you need to discard just a few items at first—as sort of a test to see if your world falls apart when that stuff is gone. Then, when it's been gone awhile and you feel okay to go on, get rid of more things.

Linda's challenge was to de-clutter her many jewelry boxes. (She owned only a few pieces of "real" jewelry; everything else was inexpensive costume baubles.) For more than three decades, she had kept the home she shared with her husband fairly clutter-free but had never disposed of even one piece of jewelry. She often bought earring-necklace-bracelet sets to go with a specific outfit, and kept the jewelry long after the clothes were gone. If she lost one earring and had no use for the remaining one, she still kept it. If she broke a necklace that could not be fixed, she

---

TOO TRUE TO ARGUE

1. Clutter begets clutter. Many people do not tend to put clutter on a clear surface, but they will happily add their contribution once a few items have been piled up.
2. The best way to keep house is to have fewer belongings to keep.
3. We all have stuff that we love—for a while—and then one day, instead of looking wonderful, it looks like clutter.
4. De-cluttering makes things messier at first. You will need to pull everything out and go through it—whether working with a closet, a wallet, or a desk drawer.

---

kept it. If a bracelet was too snug and uncomfortable to wear, she kept it.

Every year, for her birthday and holidays, Linda asked for the same gift: a jewelry box. She described her bedroom as "Jewelry Boxes R Us." Every surface held an assortment of jewelry boxes. When people commented on her collection, she explained that she collected not boxes but jewelry. She just loved buying jewelry. Yet she had so much jewelry—stored in so many boxes—that she couldn't keep track of what she owned. When she searched for a specific item, she could never find it, so she'd buy another.

Linda's clutter-busting strategy was to go through one or two boxes every evening when she was listening to music. All she was able to throw out at first were broken fragments, a few pieces she never liked, and two jewelry boxes that she didn't need or like anymore. That was not much, but it was the best she could do.

As months went by, she found it easier to locate some of her cherished pieces and was delighted to be reacquainted with a few favorites from the past that she'd forgotten about. So she decided to go through all the jewelry again and get rid of some earring-necklace-bracelet sets that she knew she'd never wear again. It was clear that she could not throw these "old friends" away; after asking around, she learned that one of her coworkers belonged to a church ministry helping welfare recipients land jobs. Clothes and accessories were especially needed. Once Linda knew that her jewelry would be appreciated and used, she found it easy to donate two or three sets at a time through her colleague at work.

When a neighbor invited Linda to join in a garage sale, she put out lots more jewelry and jewelry boxes. Linda made a few bucks and moved out about half her jewelry. She plans to dispose of more pieces in the future.

Now that she finds it easier to say good-bye to her gems, she laughs remembering what a struggle she had with her first clutter-busting session.

A SMART STRATEGY

Store frequently used items in convenient spots
(not up high or too far back).
If your kitchen counter is cluttered with appliances and gadgets, assess how often you use each item. Although most people use their electric can opener often, use of a blender, food processor, or mixer varies, according to your cooking routines. Whatever you use infrequently, such as a waffle iron, should not take up valuable counter space. This sort of thing could be tucked in one of your hard-to-reach spots.

Match up similar items.
If you have discovered five containers of nutmeg and twelve sets of lights in the shape of red chili peppers, it's probably because you haven't grouped similar items. Doing so prevents duplicating those funny little oddball things that we forget we already own.

GATHER, DON'T SCATTER

After attending one of my seminars, Robb realized that keeping similar items together, which sounds so simple and logical, is a habit that was never adopted at his house. He called me to report: "The catcher's mitts are with the toys, and the bats are in the shed, and nobody ever knows where the baseballs are.

"When my wife was getting ready to bake some muffins, she asked me to get a few things for her. The measuring cups were at one end of the kitchen, the muffin tins were at the other end, and the paper muffin cups were in the highest cabinets, which my wife can't even reach. And she bakes muffins for us a lot.

"When either of us wants to pay bills, everything we need is scattered all over. I can't believe that we keep the spray antibacterial bottle downstairs and the Band-Aids upstairs. So *every single time* that one of our kids gets a cut, I have to run up and down the stairs while my wife comforts the child. It never occurred to me how much easier it would be to keep all the first-aid supplies together.

"I'm doing a lot of rearranging and reorganizing now."

When you decide to rearrange and reorganize, see if you can keep everything you need for certain activities in the same spot—even if it means you have to buy a second pair of scissors or roll of tape. These duplicates don't contribute to clutter but simply make your life easier.

Arrange a happy home—"a place for everything"—for what you keep.

All your possessions need a home to live in. When you're deciding where something should live, consider:

1. How often is it used? Why keep the slow cooker out if you use it only once a year?

2. Who uses it? If your kids use something regularly, let them determine the best home for it (as long as it doesn't interfere with anyone else).

3. Where do you use it? It might not seem logical to others, but if you want to keep your dental floss in the same drawer as the TV remote because you floss while watching TV, then do it.

4. When do you use it? Do you have a place to store off-season items?

5. Do you need more than one?

Remove those items that belong elsewhere.

Did you ever notice that once you sort through your clutter, there's always one stack of stuff in the corner: clothes to be put away or washed, papers to be filed, and items to be returned elsewhere? If left in the corner, the pile will spill over and gradually make its way back where it started, and your time sorting through it will become a wasted effort. Accept the fact that when you clutter-bust, you have to take the next step and put items in their happy home.

Train yourself to put everything in its place.
A good habit is as easy to form as a bad one, so cultivate the simple habit of putting things away when you finish with them.

CHOOSING WHERE TO TAKE THE PLUNGE

Should you start with your easiest clutter challenge or the hardest? The most hidden or the most visible?

When Alice was converting from her life of clutter, she decided to start with the most public place: her kitchen. Paper was piled so high on her counters, her brother joked that if she ever sold the house, her counters would look brand-new because dust and dirt never made it down to the countertop.

Many people choose to start in the living room because that's where they entertain, and as soon as it's de-cluttered they want to invite over a close friend or relative to celebrate one "clutter-free zone" in the house.

One woman told me that whenever someone visited her, she stashed all her paper and other clutter into her bedroom and closed the door. As a result, she had stacks of stuff piled everywhere—some stacks were four and five feet high—and every night when she'd try to relax and fall asleep, all that clutter would bother her. So she decided to start clutter-busting her bedroom first.

A "You've Got Clutter" Quiz

Where do you want to start de-cluttering first? The place that is:

    A. easiest
    B. hardest
    C. most hidden (caged)
    D. most public (kitchen, living room)
    E. most stress producing
    F. most expensive (bills get lost, are never paid, or you
       pay late fees)
    G. most embarrassing
    H. interfering with your work
    I. keeping you from inviting company over
    J. hassling your life the most

You already know that there's no one correct answer. If you answered yes to one of the above, you've made the right decision.

DE-CLUTTERING HABITS LEAD TO A CLUTTER-FREE LIFESTYLE

You don't have to strive to do everything suggested in this book, but you will see enormous changes if you start to cultivate just a few simple habits (see the box below). You'll be able to find what you want, and putting things away will become a part of your routine. An added bonus is all the great and wonderful things you can start using again now that you know what you have.

CULTIVATE A SIMPLE HABIT

- Don't hang on to something if you never need, use, or think about it.
- Stop bringing in more clutter.
- Find a place for everything.
- Put everything in its place *now*.
- Decide right away what to toss, what to keep, and where to keep it. If in doubt, toss it out.

EXTRA CREDIT

1. List some rewards that will motivate you to de-clutter.

   _____

   _____

   _____

   _____

   _____

   _____

   _____

   _____

2. Select one area that you would like to de-clutter. Over the next three days, devote one hour per day to that area. (Use a timer. If you don't have a timer, go out and buy one.) Put down this book and put in your first hour NOW. It's time to START SMART.

3. When you finish clutter-busting one area, you're likely to celebrate, be proud of yourself, take a break . . . and probably forget about your good intentions to de-clutter another area. So decide ahead of time what

your next project will be once this one is complete.
Write it down: _____

_____

If you really want to feel organized, select a new clutter-busting project every other month. (That schedule gives you plenty of time to complete each project.) For example, in January you will clutter-bust your desk; in March you'll attack the kitchen counters; and in May you will clear the bedroom floor.

4. Today, start to live by this simple rule: A place for everything, and everything in its place.

5

Caution!
Incoming Stealth Clutter

There must be more to life than having everything.
—*Maurice Sendak*

Once you've eliminated much of your clutter, and found a happy home for whatever is left, you're well on the way to having your clutter under control. Now you need to learn how to keep it from returning, to stop it from breaking free and becoming wild clutter again.

Stealth clutter can sneak up on you after you've worked hard to clear out and eliminate your jumble. Everything looks neat and tidy; then, in no time at all, you've got new clutter. If this should happen, don't be discouraged. This chapter will alert you to the seven causes of incoming stealth clutter and provide solutions for keeping it at bay.

1. "I'll Stick It in That Stack Till Later"

You've sorted through your clutter, got rid of most of it, and established happy homes for everything that's a keeper . . . except for one stack of stuff that, for some reason, you can't bring yourself to put away now. Maybe there are odds and ends that need to be filed, mended, taken to the basement or garage, or put away behind the boxes on the top shelf in your closet. You're exhausted from all your hard work and tempted to leave that stack "till you get time." The trouble is, you never have time to finish de-cluttering unless you make the time. If you leave the stack in the corner, soon you've got clutter again.

Solution: I wish everyone, as they attack their clutter, could have a sign hanging nearby that reads:

SIT AND SORT

STAND AND DELIVER

If you're going to conquer your clutter, you *must* take that stack (which always seems to be there in the end) and deliver it to where it belongs.

Taylor had stacks of stuff left over at the end of every clutter-busting session. Whether she was clearing papers off her desk or oddball items that had accumulated in the guest bedroom, there was always one or more stacks of things that belonged someplace other than there.

She used to just leave those stacks for a lot of reasons; sometimes she was tired of working or of making decisions; sometimes she just ran out of time or had to drive her children some-place. And the stacks would all flow back to where they started, so the next time she looked, her clean, clear area looked clut-tered again. She'd feel frustrated because then she had to start all over.

Now if she has one hour to spend clutter-busting, she'll set the timer to go off in about forty minutes. She'll spend the re-maining twenty minutes delivering recipes to the recipe box in the kitchen, returning a shovel to the garage, and putting a box of donations in the front seat of her car so she'll remember to drop it off on the way to work. The best lesson she learned was that it's better to bring one small area to completion than to do larger-scale de-cluttering and have leftover stacks all over the place.

2. "WHY DOES IT FEEL LIKE I'M ALWAYS RUMMAGING?"

Did you ever straighten out a drawer, a purse, a suitcase, and the very next time you needed something, you found yourself shuf-fling and snuffling and pawing through the contents like a pig rooting in the mud? Everything inside ended up in a jumble with the definite look and feel of clutter.

There may be some people who can dig deep down into a giant drawer of sweaters, pull out the one they want from the very bot-tom, and leave all the other sweaters still stacked and neatly folded. But I'm not one of those people . . . and nobody in my family is. We are all rummagers, and I suspect most people are.

Solution: Every family has rummagers, and every home has spots that invite rummaging; it's hard to stop rummagers from doing their thing. But there's a saying that if you can't take the wind out of somebody's sails, then just lower the sail. How? Here are some ideas:

- Does searching for a measuring spoon or spatula in a kitchen drawer drive you mad? Get everything possible *out* of that drawer—especially items you use all the time. Hang measuring cups and spoons on cup hooks inside cabinet doors. (If you have young children who help you put away these items, use a lower cabinet within your kids' reach.)
- Stick spatulas, wire whisks, pancake flippers, and wooden spoons in a vase, pitcher, or jar next to the stove. These two steps alone can liberate almost a whole drawer full of rummaged stuff, without adding a look of clutter to the counter.
- Instead of tossing everything in a purse that has only one section, where you rummage every single time you need something, buy purses with divided sections and cultivate the simple habit of putting certain items in certain spots all the time. I find that purses with the same dividers come in all shapes, styles, and colors.
- Hang T-shirts, jeans, and even sweats in the closet so you can see what you want to wear, instead of having to dig to the bottom of a drawer for it and leaving everything in shambles. (Don't worry; by the time you

How to Pack a Rummage-Proof Suitcase

Kort used to hate living out of a suitcase when she traveled because after taking out the first item, everything else became rumpled and jumbled up. But she also hated wasting time unpacking. There were never enough hangers at the hotels, and trying to hang up everything was a pain in the elbow.

She developed a packing system that works like a charm *and* completely eliminates all rummaging. It requires a suitcase with a loop for hanging clothes. When she packs the suitcase, she puts whatever she can on hangers—even her nightgown and her swimsuit coverup—and places other items in one-gallon plastic storage bags (for example, socks in one, underwear in another, panty hose in another). When she gets to the hotel, it takes less than a half a minute to swoop all the hanging clothes into the closet and sweep all the plastic bags into a drawer. Packing to go home is equally simple and quick.

read chapter 8, which addresses closet clutter, they'll all fit in your closet because you'll have lots more room than you do now.)

- Put a hanging organizer with pockets in your closet and keep your panty hose or socks in each pocket.
- Hang long necklaces on cup hooks inside the closet door. Or if you have really nice ones, why not display them? Sue nailed about twenty tiny finishing nails into two feet

of one-half-inch molding, nailed that to the bedroom wall, and hung many of her beautiful necklaces on it. She never has a problem finding or untangling them, and they look terrific on the wall.

Do you see how this storage style prevents even the most dedicated rummager from making a jumble of items? Notice where and what gets rummaged and see if you can figure out a way to head it off at the pass.

3. "I'm Just Too Busy to Put Things Away"

If you think you don't have time, the problem may be that you don't have a realistic idea of how much time is required. You might believe that it would take you so long to put something away that you'd be late for work; the reality could be that the whole "putting-away process" takes less than a minute.

Solution: Get a stopwatch or a watch that counts off seconds. Then perform a few "anti-clutter" activities and time them. For example, go into the bathroom and time how long it takes to put the cap on the tube of toothpaste and place it where it belongs, and hang up the towel. Or go into the bedroom and time how long it takes to sling a shirt on a hanger and to fling clothes into a clothes hamper. No clothes hamper in the bedroom? Well, maybe that would be part of the solution to this problem. Buy a clothes hamper for every room where people remove clothes. Also buy a wastebasket for every room where clutter ap-

pears, and see if that might stop some of that stealth clutter from sneaking under your radar.

Kym keeps a large wastebasket in the garage right next to where her car ends up. As she exits the car, she looks around for any trash (such as papers or empty cans or bottles) and tosses it into the wastebasket before grabbing the groceries or briefcase or packages. That wastebasket was a great investment; it makes it easy for Kym to keep her car fresh and neat looking.

Change your attitude about how long a clutter-busting activity actually takes. When we are rushing around like maniacs, we need to remind ourselves that a thirty-second pause to pick up something or to put something away will have no impact on our time in the long run but will have an enormous impact on our clutter and sense of well-being.

The following words of wisdom are from a plaque that hangs in my neighbor's kitchen.

IF YOU WEAR IT, HANG IT UP.
IF YOU DROP IT, PICK IT UP.
IF YOU EAT OUT OF IT, WASH IT.
IF YOU SPILL IT, WIPE IT UP.
IF YOU TURN IT ON, TURN IT OFF.
IF YOU OPEN IT, CLOSE IT.
IF YOU MOVE IT, PUT IT BACK.
IF YOU BREAK IT, REPAIR IT.
IF YOU EMPTY IT, FILL IT UP.
IF IT RINGS, ANSWER IT.
IF IT HOWLS, FEED IT.
IF IT CRIES, LOVE IT.

4. "I NEVER THINK TO DO THAT"

Have you noticed that when meetings are regularly scheduled for the first Monday of the month or for every other Thursday, you find it easier to attend them? You plan for them, remember them, and work your schedule around them. Attendance becomes automatic—a habit. It's the same with maintaining a clutter-free environment. Setting some sort of regular schedule for a clutter-busting project will help you remember to do it.

Mary goes through her cluttered shelves of food once a year, in May, when the post office asks the public to put out by their mailboxes nonperishable food items for local food pantries. Not only does she buy a load of canned goods to donate, but she also drags out everything from the food shelves and donates whatever "mistakes" she bought that the family isn't eating. For example, a new soup came out that she was sure her family would love, so she bought eight cans. Then, in May, she donated seven of the cans to the post office's food drive.

Like Mary, you can tie in some of your clutter-busting-patrols with a date, season, or routine. For example:

- At the start of every summer and winter, go through your clothes closet and decide what to keep and what to dispose of. Get rid of clothes that you don't like anymore, that don't fit, that were a mistake to buy in the first place—in short, clothes that you know you'll never wear again. Help your children establish this habit, too.
- Scan clothes while folding laundry to decide what stays and what goes.
- Glance through magazines and catalogs during TV commercials.
- At the beginning of each season, go through your pantry and cabinets and get rid of whatever you won't use. Donate it to your favorite food pantry.

- Cultivate the simple habit of going through your purse and/or wallet and your car every weekend so you start off the week fresh and clutter-free.
- Each time you come home with groceries, dump out the food in the fridge that you know you'll never eat, before you put in the items you just bought. It's *not* a law that you have to wait till foods turn green and fuzzy before you're allowed to throw them out.

5. "HELP! THERE'S A CLUTTER CULPRIT IN OUR HOME"

What should you do if you find time to prevent clutter but *somebody else* in your home is not putting things back where they belong? What do you do with your spouse, kid, or other offender? Maybe you've tried nagging these Clutter Culprits, or arguing with them, or yelling at them. If so, you already know that such tactics won't work.

Solution: Bore them to tears. Josh handed his Clutter Culprit (his teenage son) a little spiral notebook, a pen, and a stopwatch, then said, "We have to go identify a problem. Come with me."

They walked to where clutter had accumulated on the kitchen counter. Josh asked his son to time him as he rinsed out and placed in the dishwasher a glass his son had left on the counter. The time was recorded in the notebook. Then they walked into the family room and timed how long it took Josh to pick up a glass, take it into the kitchen, and put it in the dishwasher.

Though he felt like laughing, Josh kept a straight face as they noted exactly how long each activity took. His son found this exercise to be so boring and annoying, he decided he would rather pick up after himself than endure another of Josh's "timing sessions."

Yes, I'll agree that maybe it won't work with your Clutter Culprit, but how will you know unless you try? And it *has* worked for many people. To find out how long it takes to put things back where they came from can be a startling eye-opener not only for your family, but also for you.

Another solution: When your Clutter Culprit is open to doing some de-cluttering, and he is on the fence about getting rid of something, you can be the Clutter Coach and in a kind, loving voice tell him, "You will have the memory of those three broken doorknobs. Those broken doorknobs can live in your heart forever, but now it's time to say good-bye to them."

If that causes too much separation anxiety, suggest that you pack up some of his stuff and leave it in the basement or garage for a few months. If he is comfortable living without it that long, he might agree to have you dispose of that batch of stuff. Neither of you should look inside the box; otherwise the anxiety will start all over again.

Third solution: Sometimes you can toss out someone else's clutter when that person isn't looking, and sometimes you can't. You've got to figure out this one for yourself.

Shannon, who has had some success fighting stealth clutter

with stealth clutter-busting, offers the following advice: Most true Clutter Culprits can't find half their stuff anyway, so when they're not around, you begin to dispose of it—discreetly. Don't start with clutter that is right in front of them every day. Start with the stuff they can't see that is hidden and buried under other clutter, and remove it gradually.

Sometimes Clutter Culprits will agree to get rid of clutter, but they just don't want to do it themselves or be around when it's being tossed out. Don't force them to be present during the clutter-busting. Otherwise, you'll be tossing stuff out, and they'll be right behind you dragging it all back in.

It doesn't seem fair that *you* should be stuck with getting rid of all their stuff, but this is not the time to get into "your stuff and my stuff; your job and my job." If you are capable of throwing out clutter and your Clutter Culprit is not, but is willing to let you be the tosser-outer, then seize the moment and start tossing. Sometimes that's the only way you'll ever dig out from all that clutter.

When Juanita's children grew up and moved out of her house, they became Clutter Culprits in absentia by leaving behind boxes, bikes, and all sorts of cluttery stuff.

She learned to say, "I'm trying to do without tons of stuff so there's not clutter everywhere. One way you can help is to remove your [fill in the blank] from my place, or on the fifteenth the Salvation Army is picking up everything." The first time she spoke those words, she had expected to be terrified, but it was not at all as difficult as she had feared.

A fourth solution: We can't change people who don't want to change, and some people just gotta have their clutter. In that case, give them one clutter spot that is all theirs and you promise to keep your hands off. It can be their room or closet, or their half of a room or a closet, or their office. Maybe a section of the basement or garage. They may simply need one place where they can have all their beloved clutter together. You won't clean it, won't nag about it, won't touch it, but that means it has to be a spot where you won't have to see it or step over it.

And if the clutter meanders out beyond the boundaries that you have both agreed upon, you have the right to do with it what you want. For first or second offenses, many people just stash away the captured clutter for a while and eventually return it. But if they have agreed to keep their clutter in a certain spot, and you keep finding it spread all over, you might decide on more drastic measures. The choice is yours.

6. "I'll Decide . . . Later"

More than half our clutter comes from procrastinating about decisions. We can't decide whether to keep this item, or can't decide where to put it, or just haven't decided to put it away yet. We can't decide how to respond to that e-mail. And so on and so forth.

Solution: Realize that you're not procrastinating about your clutter; you're putting off your decision making. Put up a sign, *Decide now!*

If you find yourself handling a piece of paper that you've handled many times before, or rummaging through the same drawer over and over, make a decision about it now—and take action now (file or toss the paper; identify and weed out the junk from the drawer so you can find what you're looking for).

7. "IT'S HARD TO PASS UP A GREAT BARGAIN"

I always begin my seminars on stress management with two questions: What is a major cause of your stress? How do you handle stress when it hits you?

One of the most common responses is "My biggest cause of stress is the clutter in my life. And I handle this stress by going shopping." I'll ask these respondents if they see a connection between the two. Some do, and some don't.

Another common response is "My biggest cause of stress is that I don't have enough money to pay my bills. And I handle this stress by going shopping." When I ask these respondents if they see a connection between the two, most do not.

Shopping can create clutter beyond our wildest dreams. In recent years, the most popular family activity in the United States has been going to the mall. We seldom shop for something specific. We wander up and down aisles looking for something—anything—to jump out, grab us, and yell, "Buy me! Buy me!" We are becoming a nation of megaconsumers who buy what we don't need and bring home more things than we could ever use and find places for.

When you're deciding to buy something—whether at a department store, thrift shop, or garage sale; by catalog; or on eBay—if you don't need or won't use this item and have no place to put it, are you buying it just because you like to buy?

Do you think it will make you happy? For how long?

Think back on some of the fantastic prizes you've bought in the past. Does that bargain still bring joy to you? Or do you not have a clue where you put it or whatever happened to it? Or—worse—did you spend a lot of money shopping last month, and you don't even remember what you bought? (So much for shopping making you happy.)

Some people who cannot set limits to their out-of-control spending decide to seek professional counseling. At one of my seminars, a participant told the group: "My finances are a mess. I'm embarrassed to admit how high my credit card debt is; I worry about not putting money away for our children's college or for our retirement. So I'm spending money I can't afford to buy toys my kids don't need that add to the clutter that we all hate. I need help . . . and I think I have to find a therapist."

I'll add one more question: What does that behavior teach your children?

If you are ever going to conquer your clutter, you *must* stop bringing more clutter into your life.

CULTIVATE A SIMPLE HABIT
When you buy something, get rid of something.
A tie for a tie, a shoe for a shoe.

A Variation on the Bargain Barbarian

Some people cannot pass up a bargain, but somewhere along the way, they have learned to stop bringing more clutter into their homes. So what's their solution? They buy on-sale items for other people, including you, which contributes to *your* clutter.

When Is a Good Deal Not a Good Deal?

Whether it's marked-down items the day after a holiday, or a
garage sale, or just a plain old good deal, it's *not* a good deal if it
contributes to more clutter, more chaos, and more guilt.

Some people refuse to acknowledge their weakness for a
good deal even when it's having a negative impact on their life.
Consider, for example, the story of Julie's neighbor, Katie, who
used to brag that she never, ever fell for bargains and *never*
bought anything that generated clutter in her house. (Julie believed her because Katie had a streamlined, neat house that was
free of clutter.)

Julie noticed that every Christmas Katie dreaded, complained about, and put off decorating. This seemed odd because at other times she decorated everything so beautifully. One day Julie stopped in to see her neighbor, who was finally getting started putting up her holiday beauty. Katie came to the door almost in tears and looking exhausted, and her living room was filled with boxes. She said, "I just finished lugging all these boxes down from the attic. I could decorate the whole town and still have a bunch left over."

Julie asked Katie how she ended up with so many decorations. The answer was "Well, I bought most of them for half price at those day-after-Christmas sales. You know, at my age, I've been to many, many sales. And I have thirty-seven boxes' worth to show for it."

Solution: If your collection of decorations is so large that decorating for holidays has become unmanageable, you can solve this problem by getting into the habit of streamlining your collection each time a particular holiday rolls around. Here's how: When unpacking your decorations for a holiday, you'll come across items you never use and never will use. Get rid of them right then and there, or pass them on to family members who *would* use them. (You could wrap up sentimental items such as Christmas ornaments and give them as gifts to the relatives who care about them.) When taking down decorations, get rid of some more. Eventually, the decorating will become manageable again. If you don't want this problem to recur, beware of buying decorations after a holiday is over, just because they're "too good a deal to pass up."

THE CLUTTER COP

A Clutter Cop is someone who is combating stealth clutter and asking a lot of questions when anyone in the family (including herself) is making a purchase:

- Do you really want to spend your hard-earned cash *adding* to your clutter?
- Do you really need this item . . . or just want it?
- Where will you put it?
- Can you get rid of some of the stuff you don't need or want in order to make room for new stuff?
- If you're trying to get out of debt, is this purchase absolutely necessary?
- Will this item soon become something that you don't need or want? Why are you spending money on it?

One day, you may hear someone call you the Clutter Cop. "I think most families will grumble about some of the new expectations and ways of life when the clutter is gone," observed Tanner.

"Yes, in the beginning, they called me the Clutter Cop because to keep the clutter from coming back, I did some follow-up and monitoring.

Before, it might have been unreasonable to expect our six-year-old to put away his game after playing with it, but now it's easy for him to get it in and out, and he can reach it, so it's no longer unreasonable."

Tanner went on to say, "Your reminders and follow-up result in your living in a neat, clean home, where you can feel comfortable and not embarrassed, and you're not always wasting time looking for things."

I'll add that you are also helping your family cultivate simple habits that will make their lives more serene, organized, and productive. So stick to your guns. The Clutter Cop will be appreciated one day. Everyone benefits from clutter-busting.

EXTRA CREDIT

1. If you are a shopaholic, write down the following questions on a piece of paper and wrap your charge cards in it. Read questions before every purchase:
   - Do I have a place to put this item?
   - Will I ever want it again?
   - Will I ever need it?
   - Will I ever use it?

- Am I buying it because someone might need it some-day but probably won't; or if anybody does need it, I won't be able to find it?
- Will I forget I have it?
- Do I want to actually spend my money to *add* to my clutter?

2. Before you buy for others, ask yourself:
   - Am I adding to someone else's clutter?
   - How sure am I that so-and-so would want, need, or love this?
   - Have I ever asked people what they would like me to buy them?
   - Have I ever discussed clutter with this person? Do I know how she feels about all the tchotchkes I buy for her?
   - Am I imposing my taste on other people by purchasing decorations for their homes?
   - Would other people be happier if I passed up this bargain and gave them what they really wanted?

3. Each time you refrain from an unnecessary purchase, put that money you would have spent in savings. Or just write down the amount you would have charged and watch the numbers add up.

4. Are you ready to announce to others around you that you will be the Clutter Cop watching out for incoming stealth clutter? If yes, go for it.

6

How to Handle Paper and Computer Info-Clutter

How you gather, manage, and use information
will determine if you win or lose.
—*Bill Gates*

Most likely, you generate and receive hundreds of pounds of paper a year. Books, magazines, letters, reports, printouts inform and entertain us, but we need to set boundaries. Your success does not rely on having mountains of information, but on how you select, manage, and use the small amount of information you actually need.

Is it possible for you to read and absorb all the newspapers, memos, magazines, catalogs, mail, and e-mails that come your way? Probably not. Yet how often do you feel guilty or anxious about all that you have to "get around to reading someday"? You can't read it all; you can't do it all. You must start to set limits on not only the amount of paper and online information coming into your life but also the amount of it you are trying to read and process.

Ordinary Paper Clutter

Don't you hate it when you are looking for something in your files (or shoe boxes or baskets or wherever you keep your papers), and there are so many files that you don't even know where to start looking? How much of the paper you have filed and stacked and stored do you think you ever read or refer to? Twenty percent maybe? So why are you keeping it all?

Obviously, it makes sense to throw out unnecessary papers. In some cases, we have to read the paper, glean the information we need from it, and file that information in our brain before we toss out the paper. But what if we don't remember the information when we should? Unless the paper is crucial to your life or work, toss it.

Anytime you attack paper clutter, it's a good idea to work on one small section at a time, then take a break. Why? By this point, you should know the answer: Because when you de-clutter, you have to make lots of decisions in a short period of time:

- Why do I have this piece of paper?
- Is it important?
- Should I keep it or throw it away or pass it on to someone?
- If I *do* keep it, where should I put it?
- Does the paper have any tax or legal implications? If so, saving it is justified. But keep it with other papers that have to do with tax or legal issues.
- Do I honestly believe I will *ever* need this paper?

- If I do need it, will I know where to find it?
- Should I toss it because, if necessary, I can easily obtain the same information elsewhere (for example, on the Internet, in a library file, or in a file kept by a colleague or friend)?
- Do I need to create new files to organize my papers?
- Should I create those files before I start clutter-busting or leave the job till later?
- What is the worst thing that could happen if I don't save this information?

Many people have had success working on a small section of paper clutter for one hour. They set a timer and when it dings, take a break. On the other hand, there are people who become so energized by bringing order to all this chaos that they don't *want* to stop after the hour is up. They just want to keep working on their de-cluttering project. If you want to keep working because you love getting control of all this chaotic paperwork, go for it!

To get control of paper clutter *fast*, sort all your paper into only four categories:

> **F**ile
> **A**ct
> **S**tand and deliver
> **T**oss or recycle

The File Stack

The file stack may be miles high, but at least when you're finished, everything in this stack has a home—unless you *don't* have a place to put these things. Then you must first solve that problem.

The short-term solution is to put similar items together (bills with bills, insurance papers with insurance papers, auto stuff with auto stuff, and so on) and then find temporary containers for them (such as shoe boxes or baskets) or clear off space on shelves or in drawers. Long-term solutions include any of the following:

eeek!

- Obtain a file cabinet.
- Get a desk and reserve one drawer for bills, one for receipts, one for supplies (envelopes, pens, stamps, tape, et cetera).
- Find an assortment of boxes that are the right sizes for the various categories of paper. Stack in a closet or under the bed.
- Put papers in a three-ring binder and keep the binder in a bookcase.

Once you have a place to put your papers, and once you start putting them there, you'll see your paper clutter diminish.

How do you set up a filing system? Set it up according to

your needs, not someone else's. There are many filing systems, and that's because one system does not work for everyone. Don't get forced into an organizational plan that you will grow to hate.

Kurt had a friend of his help set up his filing system. When Kurt needed to retrieve the policy for his car insurance, he searched through his files but couldn't find it. Finally, he had to call his friend. You guessed it. The papers were filed under "Auto." Kurt was looking for "Car"; he never calls his vehicle an auto.

When you go through your paper clutter, what categories keep popping up? *That's* what needs a file. Call it what you will call it when you look to retrieve it. (If it is something you will never need, look at, or refer to, toss it.) Where do you put invitations, brochures for a class you're going to take, and directions to that restaurant where you're meeting your friends next month? How about one file titled "Places I'm Going To"? Whenever you are filing something that doesn't belong in an existing category, start a new one.

The category for income tax is especially important. Justin found this out the hard way. Every year at income tax time, he used to chase around the house in a panic, trying to track down all the papers he needed. The anxiety and frustration would give him a blazing headache, and he'd end up feeling exhausted because it seemed that there were always a few expense receipts that he had to search for until almost dawn.

So he decided to set up a filing system. He got a large plastic container that held hanging files, and made a file for every type of receipt he would need at income tax time.

The system didn't work. Justin couldn't get himself to file his papers regularly, so they ended up being scattered all over the house again. Finally, his sister brought over an empty three-pound coffee can with a plastic lid. In front of Justin, she cut a slit in the lid. Then she asked him, "Do you think you can stuff your receipts in here every day or whenever you get them?" He said he could. And he did.

Then, around the middle of January, he called her and said he was receiving envelopes with statements for interest and earnings from his investments. This man, who is so smart about investments, told his sister that her system was working, but these statements didn't fit in the coffee can. She didn't laugh at him or put him down; she came to his house with a big shoe box from a pair of boots and in front of him cut a slit in the top. Then she asked him, "Do you think you can stuff your statements in here whenever they arrive?" He said he could. And he did.

Justin used that coffee can and boot box as a filing system for years, and it always worked. There were no more scattered receipts; no more panic attacks, headaches, or exhaustion from frantically searching for missing papers. He has now switched over to using the hanging files, and that system is working for him, too.

Justin also made an amazing discovery. He was under the impression that he procrastinated about doing the income tax. Not true. He put off the search for receipts and other papers. Ever since they've all been filed in one place, he hasn't dreaded doing the tax work, and some years he even starts early on the project.

When organizing and storing the papers you will need for income tax preparation, you can use any filing system or receptacles you like. (Of course, statements require a bigger receptacle than receipts do!) Then, whether you're doing the tax work or someone else is doing it for you, you will have all your papers together when you need them.

Filing systems don't have to be complicated, formal, or expensive. You just have to decide what you need, then set up a system that you can work with that will work for you.

The Act Stack

The second stack you'll make comprises papers you can't file away until you do something about them—until you *act* on them. Maybe you have to make a phone call or write a reply or gather some information or fill out an application. Each task takes only a few minutes, but you're not going to do any of them until you have finished clutter-busting. Even if you come across something wonderful you want to read that will take only a few minutes, do not read it till you've completed your clutter-busting.

If your act stack is huge, sort the papers into categories (such as bills or correspondence) and place each categorized stack in a container (such as a file folder, box, or basket). Jumbled stacks are counterproductive; categorized stacks give you easy access to documents.

Dan's act stack was a mountain that never turned into a molehill. If something was a big priority, he would have done it

HOW MUCH TIME IS YOUR
MESSY DESK COSTING YOU?

Are you always searching through piles of scattered papers? Are you often late because you can't find what you need either on your desk or in the drawers? Does the constant rummaging through all these papers make you so tense you want to bang your head against the computer screen—but there's a bunch of books and a stack of paper in front of it so you can't reach it right now?

In the book *Taming the Paper Tiger at Work*, Barbara Hemphill cites that research shows the average person spends 150 hours each year looking for misplaced information. Since the typical worker is on the job 40 hours per week, or about 160 hours per month, over the course of the year almost one month of working days is wasted—on rummaging!

If you could cut your clutter in half, you would cut those 150 wasted hours in half. It would be like giving yourself nearly two extra workweeks each year; sort of like "found money," but it would be "found time." Can you imagine what an impact that would have on your life?

You could use those extra hours any way you wish: to relax or have fun or be with those you love or, for you workaholics, to get even *more* work accomplished. Can you imagine what an impact it would have on a business if every year each employee was able to give two extra weeks of productivity by cutting clutter and rummaging in half?

already. Therefore, everything in the act stack was a fairly low priority, but one that he still wanted to complete . . . someday. When the mountain became so high that he feared it would topple, his strategy was to process five randomly selected items from the act stack each day. Once in a while, he would set aside time to prioritize the stack; then moving along items from the top assured him that he was acting on the most important projects. When he found himself repeatedly putting the same piece of paper at the bottom of the pile, he'd force himself to make a decision either to do the task now or to drop the whole idea and toss out the paper.

After you have filed your act stack, continue to sort bills, correspondence, notices, newspapers, and school papers into individual containers or folders as they come in. Immediately put them where they belong. Then, if you need a bill, you may have to rummage through several bills to find it, but that's certainly better than having to sort through every single paper in the room.

Sit and Sort; Stand and Deliver

Your third pile is the "stand-and-deliver stack." You can't just sit and sort, and be done with it. Whenever you sort through any clutter, it's inevitable that you'll end up with a stack of stuff that belongs elsewhere: recipes that belong in someone's kitchen, statements that are kept in a file cabinet in another room, papers to be returned to people, important documents to be placed in your safety deposit box. (See the list of items in the box on page 119.)

If you don't *stand and deliver* that stuff to where it belongs, it will revert to clutter scattered all over the place. You'll end up having to sort through the whole pile again. The secret is: move your body. You have to stand up and walk around delivering your papers to their proper spots.

The Toss Stack

The last category comprises items to be tossed. Any time you start organizing paper clutter, make sure you have a big, plastic trash bag or a big wastebasket at your side. (Keep a recycling container nearby too.) Don't use a teeny-tiny wastebasket. If you have megaclutter, as most people do, make sure you have megawastebaskets in every place where paper clutter gathers or where you open mail. Remember that your wastebasket is not an evil monster who eats all your important data; it is your sweet friend who needs to be fed and nourished.

When you have finished de-cluttering and you have everything in four stacks, go ahead and take out the toss and recycle papers. Then take care of the stand-and-deliver stack. Now you have only two stacks: file and act. Not so overwhelming anymore, is it?

SPECIAL CATEGORIES OF PAPER CLUTTER

One of my favorite clutter questions is Would you pay to increase your paper clutter? You probably would answer, "No, never! I hate this paper clutter. Why would I pay to add to it?" Yet that's what you're doing each time you subscribe to a "too-much-of-a-good-thing" magazine.

How do you determine what kind of magazine you have coming to you? When your magazine arrives in the mail, do you rejoice because you can hardly wait to read it? Or do you feel even more swamped than before because now you have to add one more to the six months' worth that has been waiting in the corner for you to read?

Reality check: If you have more than a three-month backlog on any magazine, reconsider why you're spending money on something you're not reading. Isn't that like throwing away cash? Is that how you want to spend your earnings?

A "You've Got Clutter" Quiz

What questions do you ask yourself when you're about to sign up for a new magazine subscription?

A. Why do I want this magazine?
B. Do I want it only for specific information pertaining to my career or hobby?
C. Do I want it only for certain—but not all—articles?
D. Do I want it only for health tips?
E. Do I want it only for recipes?
F. Do I want it only for investment information?
G. Do I plan to read each issue from cover to cover? (Many people don't *plan* to do this, but they refuse to dispose of a magazine till they've read every single word. Go figure.)

If you never ask any of the above questions, the odds are that you've got a whole mountain of unread magazines hanging around your house. That's definitely a paper problem.

Solution: Ask these questions with each magazine that enters your life. Dare to be brave and cancel some subscriptions if needed.

You've got to clarify why you are subscribing to that magazine. Are you subscribing to it to read every single word? If so, do you have enough time each month to read the entire issue of every magazine you receive? If yes, fine, there's no problem. If you don't have the time, stop and reevaluate the situation. Learn to skim your magazines, not to read every word of every article, or maybe you would be better off buying a copy at a store or newsstand every few months when you do have the time to enjoy it, rather than letting back issues accumulate and feeling guilty about that.

Are you subscribing to that magazine because it contains important information that is necessary for your career or hobby? Then set up a place to store the issues, and regardless of whether you have time to read every word, they will be available to you as reference material. If you find that all the articles are archived on a Web site, you may not even have to keep back issues.

THREE SIMPLE RULES FOR TOSSING MAGAZINES, CATALOGS, OR NEWSPAPERS

1. Your magazines (or catalogs or newspapers) belong in one designated spot. If you find a copy anyplace else, toss it out.
2. Start tossing when any stack of these gets higher than a certain number of inches. (You decide how many.) Eighteen inches seems to satisfy most people; it accommodates one week's worth of newspapers, for example, but not two.
3. Toss any magazines that are more than six months old.

David leads a busy life and never used to have time to read the magazines he subscribed to. Now he keeps three or four magazines in a carrying case he received at a conference. He's gotten into the habit of having the case with him whenever he's away from home, even when he's also lugging a briefcase of papers.

TOO TRUE TO ARGUE

Many people take out magazine subscriptions because a school is selling them as a fund-raiser, or because they are being offered as a "premium" (that is, they are free for the first few months) or as just a "good deal."

But it's not a good deal when the magazines

- clutter up the home
- cause trees to be cut down to provide paper and
- generate feelings of guilt, anxiety, and being overwhelmed because you don't have time to read them.

Sometimes it's a better deal to give the school a donation and skip the magazines.

Beware! "Free" magazines usually have a few "small fees" that over a period of time add up to several hundred dollars.

Beware! When you accept a free magazine and give your credit card number, the publisher might keep renewing your subscription *every year* unless you track down its customer-service phone number and put a stop to this.

Then, whenever he's waiting—in the car, for a train, in a restaurant for a friend or colleague to arrive, in an office for an appointment or for a meeting to start—he grabs a magazine and reads it.

He was amazed to discover how many "precious pockets of time" there are in a day, and he uses them to catch up on his favorite magazines.

Maureen does the same thing but takes it a step farther. She reads her magazines on the bus, subway, or at the doctor's office; then she tears off the address label and leaves the magazines there for others to enjoy.

Catalogs

With the first few, you were fascinated by all the gadgets. Then your name magically was sold to every catalog company this side of the equator, and now you have a catalog deluge.

Solution: Let a month's worth accumulate, and when you sit down with that huge stack, you'll find yourself carefully going through the first few, then flipping past pages of the next ones, then finally tossing out some without even looking at them. And please note that the world does not end when you do that.

Also, if you knew for sure that this catalog arrived *not* because you wanted it but because the catalog company bought your name from another catalog company, it would be easy to toss it, right? But how to know this?

Use a secret code name.

That's what Connie Johnston did. "When I ordered from a garden catalog, I used the name Lily Johnston," she said, "and can count seventeen different companies that bought that mailing list so far. In addition, I receive catalogs addressed to Gadget Johnston, Red Blouse Johnston, Kitty Cat Johnston, Nature Gal Johnston, and all sorts of other crazy code names that I've made up. It's fun, and it warns me to get rid of the catalog before I even open it."

Beloved Books

What about our beloved books? Well, we all have our weakness. I have never figured out how to give up any of my books that I cherish so much. But at least we can get rid of old textbooks and junky books that we aren't madly in love with. If you cannot throw them out, offer them to your local "Friends of the Library" for their annual sale.

A word of warning if you're tempted to add to your collection by joining a book-of-the-month club: Every few weeks the club will send you a description of new books, and unless you follow its instructions and send back a reply card *right away*, it will send you a book. And another. And another. Often these are books you don't want, will never read, and can't throw away.

Notes from School and Seminars

Some people love to learn, and their favorite "hobby" is attending seminars and workshops on all sorts of fascinating topics. If you're an avid note taker, you might have clutter if you have a stack of notes from high school, and every talk and presentation you've ever attended since. Why do you save them? Do you think someone someday will ask you for your Assertiveness notes from 1979? Do you think you will actually sit down and read through them again someday? If you wanted to refer to them, would you be able to find the reference you're looking for?

At my seminars I encourage participants to take notes if they want. This enhances learning because when you write, you are engaging another sense, over and above sight and sound. But do not keep your notes forever. When you get home, glance over them and enter any special thought, quote, or action idea into your computer or a notebook designated for this purpose. Then throw out the notes.

By reviewing your notes, and copying out whatever holds special significance for you, you'll actually retain more information than if you kept your notes stacked in a corner for the rest of your life.

Greeting Cards

Cheryl doesn't have enough closet space, even though she lives alone. That's because she has a whole closet devoted to greeting cards she's received in her life. She has twenty-two big boxes of cards.

Granted, Cheryl's case is extreme, but many of us fail to see that having a bunch of greeting cards doesn't mean that we are loved and doesn't make us feel more loved when we're lonely.

What should you do if you have way too many cards taking up

space? Select a few special ones. Then either toss the rest, cut them up for gift tags, or donate them to a group that could use them for crafts. If that would be too difficult, then scan them and save the images on a disc or in a computer file.

If it breaks your heart having to get rid of cards, cut down on receiving so many. Talk to friends and relatives about your paper clutter and suggest other options to sending cards, such as: exchanging cybercards via the computer, phoning each other, or meeting in person.

Patty could not bring herself to get rid of greeting cards, primarily for sentimental reasons but also because she knew—given the high price of cards these days—that so much cash was spent on them. So she and her husband, Tom, decided that instead of exchanging cards, they would write short letters to each other on all special occasions, including their anniversary. At least then they would be keeping something much more meaningful than store-bought cards. Some of these letters not only expressed their love for each other but also summarized their life together over the past year.

Now that Tom has passed away, these love letters have become more precious than jewels for Patty.

Business Cards

Are you really going to contact these people someday? Be clear why you would need to keep their business cards. Enter the information into your database and toss the cards. If you can't throw them out, don't leave them floating loose or crammed into a big rubber-banded blob in a drawer. Purchase a file for business cards and set up some kind of filing system. Don't file cards solely according to people's last names if when you search for them all you will remember is the person's field. If you won't remember the handyman's name, file his card under "Handyman."

Papers from Your Child's School

- Put a bulletin board in the kitchen for all important school papers (such as permission slips and report cards), lists of items you need to send to school (such as snacks), and a calendar of school events.
- Give each of your children a file folder in a file cabinet where their papers belong and can be found when needed.
- Art projects and certain papers can go in the memory box. (See chapter 2.)
- Send some of your kid's masterpieces to relatives.
- Take a photo of the child with his artwork or her science project, and keep it with the rest of your photos.
- Instead of saving essays or artwork, scan them and store on a disc or in a computer file.
- Frame artwork but rotate in new pieces and discard old ones.
- Keep the school newsletters, office memos, book write-ups, and weekly newsmagazines in a box in your car and catch up on your reading when stuck in traffic, or in a

long line at the drive-through, or while waiting to pick up the kids after school. You can take some of what's in the box in with you when you have to wait at the doctor's or dentist's office.

COMPUTER CLUTTER

Some people say that the single best paper-clutter reducer is the computer. Well, it's true that a piece of paper can be tossed once it's entered into the computer, but then what about all that computer clutter?

All of the principles for getting control of paper apply to computer clutter as well. To say that you will return to an e-mail and handle it later is exactly the same as setting down a paper on your desk and putting off that decision.

Address the following areas of computer clutter each week. Delete:

- cookies (that is, text files stored on your computer from Web sites you've visited)*
- temporary Internet files
- contents of your recycle bin for PC or trash file for Macs

*Cookies can track how often you visit a site, or save your logon name and password. Sometimes these files include graphics and sound files that gobble up a lot of computer memory.

- junk mail
- old e-mails that mean nothing to you now
- old versions of any new programs you have installed
- cartoons and goofy pictures that your friends have sent you, and anything else in your download directory you don't need

And just as with paper files, give your computer files names that mean something to you so you'll be able to retrieve them.

Another tip: If you just need to skim a file, try to do so on the screen and avoid printing it out. Otherwise, you will have added to your paper clutter.

E-mails

"I'll finish reading all my new e-mails first. Then I'll come back and reply to this one." Such a plan inevitably leads to wild e-clutter. Treat e-mail—whether at home or at work—as you would treat your snail mail.

- Delete the junk mail without opening or reading it.
- Make decisions about e-mails the minute you open them.
- Reply to every one that you can right away.
- The ones that you cannot reply to immediately should be put in an "Urgent" file so you can get to them as soon as you have the time.

- After replying to an e-mail, delete it or set up a file folder for it.
- Rather than carrying each person's e-mail to individual folders, group them in categories (friends, work, special interests, clutter tips, awaiting response)
- Don't get sucked into forwarding jokes, poems, and stories when you don't have the time to do so.
- Every time you start to write an e-mail, ask yourself, "Do I have time to do this? Is this the best use of my time right now?"

SPAM

Spam is junk e-mail you don't want to receive. If you don't know how to set up a spam filter, ask a computer-savvy friend to help you. Whether you have a spam filter or not, spam *will* get through. Turn it into a stress-management exercise.

It used to take me forty-five minutes each day to delete spam in my e-mail in-box because I didn't know any other way to handle it. At first, I found this waste of time to be frustrating and sometimes infuriating. Finally, I decided to turn it around and make it a soothing experience. As I'd go through the spam, I'd do some deep breathing and say to myself, "This e-mail stands for the stupid sink that's plugged up." Delete! "This one stands for the hassle with the cell phone company." Delete! "This one stands for the mess the raccoons made of the roof shingles." Delete! At the end of each spam session, I felt relaxed and wonderful. Now that I have a filter, I feel even more relaxed and wonderful.

You Can't Read Everything

You can't. No one can these days. Until you accept the fact that you cannot read every piece of mail, e-mail, every memo, newsletter, newspaper, magazine, and mail-order catalog that interests you, you'll be buried in clutter. The trick is to learn how to sift through and toss what you don't need, so you end up spending your valuable time on those things that are important to you.

I'm not suggesting that you throw out important or sentimental or meaningful reading material. Just the items that are cluttering up your life; that you know you'll never read or need.

And now it's time to remind ourselves that we are human and that once in a while, even with the greatest tips and techniques in the world, papers and computer clutter will accumulate. This is the twenty-first century, and clutter will be a constant battle.

EXTRA CREDIT

1. Just a reminder: Take a break at the end of every hour spent clutter-busting. (In fact, the favorite reward for most adults is *time off—guilt-free.*) Or at least pause briefly to treat yourself to something else that will recharge your battery. (Chocolate works well for many people.) One great reward you can give yourself is:

   _____

   _____

2. Post a sign, *Handle each piece of paper only once,* wherever your paper collects.
3. Make decisions about each piece of paper as it comes to you. The objective is to toss out as many papers as possible.

4. Set up folders, boxes, envelopes, drawers, or other receptacles for your papers *before* you start to attack your
paper clutter. Your choice is:

_____

_____

_____

5. Feed your wastebasket—often.

7

Home Sweet Clutter–Busted Home

There is an immediate emotional and psychological payoff to getting our houses in order.
—Sarah Ban Breathnach, *author of*
Simple Abundance: A Daybook of Comfort and Joy

Clutter-busting your home may sound like a big job, but it comes down to a few habits that are not hard to master. You will be surprised by how easily your clutter evaporates if you adopt just one, two, three, or all of these simple habits:

- Never leave a room empty-handed. Glance over your left shoulder every time you leave a room or your office. Pick up the clutter you spot, and take it with you to where it belongs.
- Never go up or down the stairs empty-handed if anything out of place belongs at the other end of the staircase.
- Become a Clutter Cop and insist that the whole family cultivate the above two simple habits. Make signs and

post them if you have to. (Tina, a teenager, has her father to thank for adopting those two habits. Every time she left a room he would holler, "Empty hands! Empty hands!" and now she feels odd leaving a room empty-handed.)

- Designate one spot for items that you buy ahead of time, such as gifts and cards. When you search for them, you'll know where to find them. With everything in one place, you won't forget what you have and buy a duplicate.
- If you have two (or more) items that serve the same function, keep the newer or better one and get rid of the others.
- Use "precious pockets of time" (during TV commercials, while on hold on the phone, while waiting for a doctor's appointment) to sort through magazines or catalogs, de-clutter your wallet or purse, process five papers that are out of place, or do any of those little things you never have time for.
- Every day, toss or put away five items that are out of place.
- If you can't put aside time to really tackle a cluttered area, every time you go past it, stop and take care of five items.
- Don't let anything come into your home unless you have a place for it.
- Start small when clearing clutter from your house. Start with one area of one room, one shelf, one drawer, one stack of papers.

- Wherever you start, decide left or right and work in that direction. That way, when you come back in a day or week or month, you can see where you left off.
- When you de-clutter a room, sort through one category of stuff at a time. First all the dishes, cups, and glasses; next the toys; then pick up papers. You get the idea.
- Select one place for each activity and keep all paraphernalia needed for that activity in that one place.
- Gather similar objects together and store them near where they are most often used.
- Invite company over once in a while. That's a terrific incentive for cleaning your house.
- Pretend you are going to move. If you were moving, would you want to keep this item, pack it, move it, unpack it, and then have to find a place for it?

KITCHEN

Here are some ideas to start de-cluttering various areas in the kitchen:

- Get rid of canisters on your counter unless you love them and use them. With most canister sets, the sugar gets hard, bugs get into the flour, and you drink only tea or coffee (not both) so one of those two is empty. Store your sugar and flour in tightly sealed plastic containers inside a cabinet, and give yourself a clear spot on your counter where those canisters used to be.

- If you have a slow cooker, empty gumball machine, waffle iron, or anything else on the counter that you use only a few times a year, tuck it away. Eventually, you'll have an uncluttered counter that makes your kitchen look larger.
- Consider how many people you have in the family versus how many glasses, mugs, dishes, and plastic sports water bottles. Sure, you need some extra for company, but do you have a lot that are never used? Do you really need all that taking up space in your cabinets?
- Cookbooks: Pull out the ones that you use; look at the ones still on the shelf. If you haven't ever used them, face the fact that you probably never will. Toss, sell, or donate them.
- Refrigerator: Sort through what's on top and on the front of the door first. Then work on the inside, starting with the door. This can be a yucky, disgusting project. Plan to give yourself a very cool reward when you're through.
- Gather similar objects together. Assign a certain spot for groups of food such as salad dressing or jams. Put all short dairy products (butter, margarine, yogurt, cottage cheese) on one short shelf. You don't *have* to use the butter compartment for butter; put something else there if you prefer.
- Murphy's Law of the Kitchen is that the *least* used items are usually smack-dab in front of the *most* used ones. With each item ask, "How often is this used?" Not often? Store

it high or low. Don't put the *most* used items in the *least* convenient spots.

- Where is the item used? Store it nearby in a place convenient to its use.
- Always decide where to keep a new kitchen item as soon as you bring it home; or better yet, *before* you even purchase it or decide to bring it home.

ENTRY AREA (ANYWHERE THAT SHOES, BACKPACKS, AND JACKETS LAND)

As people enter, do they stumble over backpacks, shoes, and a mountain of mail? So here are some tips:

- Provide boxes for boots, scarves, and gloves, or pegs for coats and backpacks. Give each person one and let her label or identify her own.
- Assign a box for each pet or for general pet supplies.
- Put an old bookcase in the entry and label a shelf for each family member.

BEDROOMS

- Buy as many wastebaskets and clothes hampers as you need, and put them where you need them. Why have the clothes hamper in the bathroom if you take off your clothes in the bedroom?

- Make "empty space" part of your decorating philosophy. Keep the tops of dressers and all other furniture as clear as possible. If you have a gazillion figurines on your dresser, try packing them away for the summer to ease your dusting chores during the hot weather. If you miss them, bring them back. There's a chance you won't miss them.

Living Room/Dining Room/Family Room

These seem to be the rooms where people gather for conversation, seated leisure-time activities, and visiting with friends. And these rooms tend to be messy. But if you have a place for everything, you can teach family members that either they put stuff where it goes, or you will gather up what's out-of-place and do something drastic with it. (Sell it, give it away, toss it, or hide it for a while.)

If you have craft projects that you *know* you'll never work on, let alone complete, or even some that are partially complete, donate them to a nursing home. They will be loved and appreciated *and* probably completed . . . finally.

Bathroom

Are you determined to clean out and organize your bathroom medicine cabinet or vanity once and for all? Here's what you need to do:

- Take everything out of the cabinet(s). Have a big bag or box ready for toss-outs and another one for donating all those gifts of bath stuff that you never use and those itty-bitty bottles of shampoo and other odd things you've picked up over the years.
- Make three stacks: one for items that should be in the cabinet(s), one for those that should be housed elsewhere, and one for outdated or unused items you can pitch.
- Check expiration dates of medications. Toss medications when they have expired, because they are no longer effective and in some cases are even toxic.
- Throw out cosmetics, face creams, and lotions that have exceeded their shelf life of about six months. Nail polish that is too hard to go on the brush needs to be tossed, too, no matter how much you love the color and can't find it anymore.
- Toss the duplicates of any item or items over six months old (especially if you haven't needed or used it).
- You have one head; why are you keeping more than one hair dryer, curling iron, etc.? Do they both work? If yes, why did you buy another one? Get rid of all but the one you use the most.
- When you put everything back into a cabinet, arrange all your supplies in a logical way. If it's a his-and-hers cabinet, divide your individual items either by shelf or use one side for his and one side for hers. Put similar items together (tooth stuff here, nail stuff there).

- Don't stack items on top of one another, or everything will fall out when you need something from the bottom. (The same advice applies to linen closets or any other place in which you stash and store stuff.)

Many of the items we put in our medicine cabinets or vanities are not the things we *choose* to put in there. These items get shoved in there just because they are little and the medicine cabinet, especially, seems to be the safe place to shove little things.

Ray sent me a list of what was in his medicine cabinet: "Besides everything I think belongs in my medicine cabinet, when I cleared it out, I found cigarette lighters (I don't smoke), about a thousand safety pins, transparent tape, buttons, loose change, golf balls (they fall out when somebody other than me opens it, so I can hear who is snooping), sunglasses, matches, rubber bands, an old audiocassette tape, metal tabs from beer cans, and several extra keys that don't fit anything but I could never throw them out.

"Rita, you'll be happy to know I threw out everything (the keys were very emotional to get rid of) except the golf balls. I think they are a pretty good 'Snoop Alarm.'"

HELPING KIDS BECOME CLUTTER-BUSTERS

Your children need and deserve to have order in their lives. They blossom in a clutter-free environment. To ask them to clean up

a room stuffed with stuff and a closet so jammed that you can't see or sort anything is an exercise in futility.

Children feel just as overwhelmed with clutter as we do, but they don't know what to do about it. So their idea of cleaning is to stuff and stash and hide, cramming things with hopes that you won't notice. You do, and you reprimand them.

To help them de-clutter their rooms is one of the kindest gifts you can give them. You will help make their living space manageable and break that negative cycle of frustration and futility that a cluttered space generates.

Do your own de-cluttering first, but let your children know what's happening. Share your struggles with them. Tell them about getting rid of those items you thought you couldn't do without. Tell them about how you feel seeing open spaces appear and clutter disappear. Share your excitement, joy, relief, feelings of freedom, or whatever. The hope is that they will *want* you to help them de-clutter their closets and rooms when they see how the rest of the house is changing for the better.

Sandra wanted to get her kids on board in clearing their house of clutter. "I wanted to reduce the clutter in our home, and I knew if the children were not on my side, it would never happen," she explained. "Many times before, I tried to 'raise the bar' in keeping our home neat, but those kids just limboed right under it."

So she decided to start by clearing a spare room in the basement, and she asked each of her four children, one at a time, to give her a hand. Typically, the teenager, Randi, decided to "give her a hand" by applauding, and the others just laughed and made jokes. Finally, after much joking, begging, and groveling, Sandra persuaded her eight-year-old daughter, Shayna, to take pity on her, and together they sorted and tossed. They both thought the project would take months and were surprised to be finished after three cleaning sessions.

Sandra was delighted, and to celebrate she took her daughter out to lunch and a shopping spree. When Shayna showed her siblings her new swimsuit, suddenly they all became interested in helping their mother.

Randi was recruited to help clear Sandra's closet because she is the oldest of the four and knows the most about clothes and what looks good on Mom. Sandra made it clear that this wasn't a job or a punishment; anytime the kids helped, they could simply sit with a soda and just cheer her on. She explained that she needed a lot of encouragement to get rid of the things that she had no use for and never used, but which she found hard to part with.

After she finished her own clutter-busting, Sandra planned on asking her children if they wanted her help with their clutter, but she wanted to wait at least two weeks. Otherwise, she feared she'd seem manipulative. But she was surprised that within days, Randi asked Sandra to go through her closet with her. They played music (with Randi introducing her mom to her's), chatted, bickered over decisions, and because Sandra's attitude was loosey-goosey instead of high-pressure, they had a good time. Again, when the project was completed, Sandra had a celebration with her daughter and a bit of a shopping spree.

When Sandra asked, "Who's next?" the others just went along with the clutter-busting. Two of the girls helped each other. After everyone felt they had de-cluttered their bedrooms and closets as much as possible, the whole family had a garage sale, ending with a pizza party and watching a favorite DVD.

When you have the kids help you with your clutter, make a big deal about saying good-bye to some of your old favorites. Pretend to cry when throwing out your junky, smelly sneakers or slippers. Blow kisses, act as if you're leaving a dear friend. Let the drama flow. This helps them understand that even though it's not easy to say good-bye to old things, it's still necessary. Your acting job might open them up to getting rid of their own clutter.

Sandra used that tactic, and even now, years later, her kids will make a big deal out of bidding a fond farewell when they decide to get rid of some of their excess stuff. The good news is that even though the house still occasionally sinks into a clutter mode, it is never as bad as it once was.

Here are some great clutter-busting tips for you and your children:

KID TIPS

Simplify the job. Make it easier for kids to be clutter-free.

- Cleaning their rooms requires kids to make decisions, and the more you help your child to simplify, the easier the cleaning and decision making become.
- Make sure that toys, books, puzzles, and games are stored in places that a child can get to easily. If he can't reach the storage area, the items will end up where you don't want them.
- Roommates handle their shared space better if clear boundaries are established: This is Meghan's drawer and this is Cassidy's drawer; or this is Connor's shelf and this is Noah's shelf. Sometimes labels are needed to help keep things straight.
- Help kids get drawers and the closet to a state where they can easily fit their clothes and other belongings into them.
- Clear off stuff that's on top of furniture.

- Some children have an extra bed in their room "for sleepovers." But most friends know to bring a sleeping bag and pillow when they spend the night. Space is too valuable to waste on a spare bed that just collects clutter. Unless the extra bed is used frequently, sell it or give it away to someone who will use it. If you really feel an extra bed is necessary, try a trundle bed, where the mattress slides under the bed.

Provide helpful items that enable a child to stay organized.

- Furnish containers of various sizes to corral toys and other items.
- Let children help label containers. (They will then be more open to using them.) They can be as creative as

they want, using either words or pictures. Or take photos of the child showing what goes in each container. Encourage your child to have fun with this hamming it up, or pretending that she's in a TV show or commercial.

- Put clothes hampers (or baskets or boxes) in each child's room. Any dirty clothes not in the hamper don't get washed.
- To simplify organizing children's laundry, try assigning a color to each child for towels, sheets, and blankets.
- Make it easy to keep clothes neat. Put shoe boxes without lids in drawers to help keep clothes from getting jumbled. Socks could go in one shoe box, for example, underwear in another. You can use any kind of container, but if you are a true Clutter Glutton and still have every shoe box that you've ever brought home, this is a good way to make use of them.
- Put a larger container (box or basket) on the closet floor for shoes, flip-flops, and slippers and another one for sports equipment, art supplies, Barbie dolls, or whatever.

Permanently reduce the amount of stuff your child could accumulate by trying some of the following techniques. Let your children see how you're getting rid of your own stuff. Then, when helping them de-clutter, give children the opportunity to decide what stays and what goes. If they can get rid of only a few things at first, so be it.

- When your child receives new toys, help him select old ones to clean up and donate to charity. Children love the feeling of helping others.
- Check out books from the library; buy only books your children really love and will read over and over again.
- Don't become a member of a children's book-of-the-month club or toy-of-the-month club without letting the club know each month whether you want that month's selection. Otherwise you'll end up with books and toys your kids don't want and won't use. It goes without saying that if you want to reduce the number of books and toys in the house, you won't join one of these clubs in the first place.
- Pack away certain toys, puzzles, and books that you bring out only during special times:

  - when a babysitter comes.
  - for a long car ride.
  - on a rainy day.
  - on a sick day or school vacation day.
  - when your child just needs his or her spirits lifted.

- Teach your children to question the need to keep broken toys, tired stuffed animals, books with torn pages or covers, or games with broken or missing pieces. Especially if they are no longer interested in these things.
- Encourage kids to contribute items to the donation container that you've set up for the family.

CREATIVE STORAGE

"Any time you can think of a creative way to store something out of sight, or to make another cage for caged clutter, go for it," advises a workshop participant. "For example, in all the bedrooms, store the extra set of sheets and extra blanket between the mattress and box spring. Same for the hide-a-bed. If you have *way* too many sheets to store under the mattress, well, what do you need all those sheets for?

"Our lives overflow with variety; we don't need six sets of sheets to add variety to our drab, dismal lives. Three sets cover it (one on the bed, one in the wash, one for emergencies). With a bunch of kids' beds, you don't need an emergency set for each child.

"Yes, if you fold them into a small neat package that is seven inches high, it *will* be lumpy. So just fold them four times or once more if it's a huge sheet. Lift the mattress and tuck in the folded sheets. Doing this freed up a whole linen closet, which was room I desperately needed for other things."

Other storage tips:

- Slide items under the bed.
- Hang them inside cabinet or closet doors.
- Store them in a trunk that serves as a coffee table.
- Hang shelves above a desk to hold books or other items.
- Use plastic containers or boxes to hold files, papers, craft material, art supplies; use large boxes as tables.

Finally, after working together as a family to de-clutter, hold a mini-celebration after clutter-busting for one solid hour (ignoring everything else and taking no breaks). Or have a big celebration when you've completed the job.

EXTRA CREDIT

1. Take photos or videos of all your clutter before you get started. You won't regret it. Great fun!
2. Celebrate *every* victory, no matter how small (for example, a clean shelf, a stack gone from the floor). Your cause to celebrate is: _____

   _____

   _____

3. Ways to celebrate include visiting with a friend, taking guilt-free time off, watching a favorite movie, spending an evening reading trashy magazines. Your way to celebrate this time is: _____

   _____

   _____

4. Buy wastebaskets and clothes hampers for every place in your home that needs them. My office has two huge wastebaskets.

8

Caged Clutter—Out of Sight and Out of My Mind

Success is having what you want;
happiness is wanting what you have.
—anonymous

The problem with caged clutter—all those things you never need or use that you stash in a drawer, closet, spare room, garage, shed, basement, or attic—is that since it doesn't have to be moved when company comes over, it can stay "as is" forever. Everyone deserves to have some caged clutter, to tuck away a few items somewhere, but this is not the same as cramming stuff to the ceiling in the garage, basement, attic, shed, spare room, and every closet and drawer in your life. You need to streamline your caged clutter.

Some people need more cages than others—especially those whose work or hobby involves collecting many items. (Some of these hobbies include art, crafts, cooking, gardening, and sewing.) Maura, an artist, defended her caged clutter in a letter she wrote to me: "Many artists have tons of clutter stored away.

Everything that is packed away in boxes is just a reflection of what artists have in their minds, and those who keep these things—old magazines, bits of articles and paper, ancient books, old toys, etc.—are aware that sometimes amongst the boxes and dust, are stimuli to beautiful and interesting ideas, which through constant shuffling and rummaging, can be transformed into something very rare and precious. Well, that's my story and I'm sticking to it!"

Yes, artists and other creative types may need extra cages for those items that nurture their passion, but as with everything else in life, they must set boundaries on their caged clutter.

Doris came up with a new category: temporary caged clutter. She wrote: "We run a business out of our home and many times I'm in the middle of opening and sorting mail and bills and things that can not be 'caged' anywhere when people stop in for a visit. If I tried to hide the mess, I'd get frustrated later because it takes me two hours to get back to where I was before I caged the papers. I now just cover the dining room table (aka my office) with a tablecloth."

CLOSETS

The expression "Less is more" never meant anything to me until I applied it to closets. When you have a closet so jam-packed that you can't slide a hanger even a quarter of an inch, doesn't it seem that you usually wear the same eight or nine items over and over? But once you clear out that closet, and the contents have room to roam, and you can see everything in there, you can wear everything in that closet. It's as if you've been on a glorious shopping spree, all for free.

Before attacking your jam-packed closet, you need to tell yourself something very important: "We all make mistakes. I am human; I make mistakes." That outfit you bought six years ago that you never wore; you will never, ever wear it. You made a mistake. Admit it. Get rid of it. Move on.

Don't decide to keep an item just because you paid a fortune for it. Keep it only if you love it, it fits and looks great on you, and it's not so out of style that people will laugh at you when you wear it.

T o o   T r u e   t o   A r g u e

If you think that you cannot possibly get along without your disco shirt or that prom dress from the dark ages, that means you won't give them up. You'll continue to struggle with a jam-packed closet of smashed-together clothes, not being able to see or find 80 percent of them. Those old clothes are not your happy memories; nor are they the happy times of a younger, more carefree you. All of that is in your heart and in your mind.

"I'm cultivating new habits and breaking some old ones," reported Jennifer. Instead of going on frequent and expensive shopping sprees, she said, "when I get the urge to splurge I head for my closet and take out an armload of clothes that I haven't worn since before computers were born. I try everything on.

Then I get rid of anything (even if it was a gift) that I wouldn't love enough to buy, and I can start wearing again those clothes that I do love."

Tanya said, "I used to keep all my clothes that don't fit anymore because I 'might need them later,' like all those too-small clothes I was saving for 'when I lose some weight.' Then I asked myself, 'Will I really wear them? Will they still be in style? If I work hard at losing the weight, and become slender and svelte, won't I feel I deserve some wonderful new clothes?' Now they've all been passed on to people who will wear them *now*."

"When our clothes become faded or ripped," observed Gretchen, "we save them to wear while painting the house, or doing yard work. We all need an outfit or two for doing grubby chores, but I realized that my husband and I had enough grubby outfits to clothe a small third-world country. We had more grubbies than wearables. So I took that as a sign that something's got to be done. That's when I knew it was Closet Clearing Time."

Here are some tips for taming closet clutter:

- Select one small area of the closet to clear (one section of clothes, the floor, or a shelf).
- Take everything out.
- Sort clothes, accessories—everything—into the following categories: *keep* (goes back in), *toss* (goes in trash), and *donate or sell* (goes in a container) or *pack*. (Don't get carried away with the last one. Wherever you pack it away to, I'll be bugging you to clear *that* out soon.)
- No category for undecided is permitted. Make your decisions now. If you don't wear it, get rid of it.
- Ask yourself: "How often do I wear this item? Does it still fit? Have my tastes changed? Do I like it and feel good when I wear it? Why am I keeping it?"
- The first few times you tackle your closet, enlist the help of a friend or relative. Offer in return to help him or her with a closet clutter-busting spree or to treat him or her to lunch. Be cautious of recruiting your teenager. Some work out wonderfully, but others, who think their parents' clothes are weird, want them to dump everything.

- Memento clothes should be just a few special items, not everything you once wore but never wear now. Pack away mementos. Don't use up valuable closet space unless you are one of the rare people who has an abundance of closets.
- Store similar clothes together (dressy, casual, or work clothes).
- Resist impulse buying. Before making a purchase, think about your wardrobe: Do you really need this item? Will it go together with any of your other clothes? Is it in a color that looks good on you?
- Store off-season clothes in suitcases shoved under the bed.
- If boxes (or anything else) are blocking the way to a closet, blaze a path through to the closet so you can start using it regularly.
- Repair the closet door. You're not likely to use a closet if you can't get to it or open the door easily.
- Store items in see-through plastic boxes so you can see what's inside.
- For kids' closets, make sure they can reach the items they need. Hang a low bar for the clothes they wear frequently and put off-season or dressy clothes on a high bar.

THE GLOVE COMPARTMENT

Empty out everything from the glove compartment. Then put back only:

- your auto-insurance card with the company's emergency phone number
- a copy of your health-insurance card
- a copy of your roadside-assistance phone number
- maps of areas where you frequently drive
- the car's owner's manual
- a first-aid kit, travel-size wipes, and tissues (optional)

THE SPARE ROOM

Ken used to wish with all his heart that he had a spare room. "In my fantasies," he explained, "it would sometimes be a guest room and at other times it would be my office, or private getaway room where I could close the door on my family and in blissful peace read or exercise or just be alone.

"They say, 'Be careful what you wish for. You might get it.' Suddenly, into my life one day a spare room came. It was wonderful, marvelous, a genuine wish-come-true. But then, that same day, I held something in my hand (can't remember what) and thought, 'Now, where am I going to put this? Oh, I know—in the spare room.'

"And in the blink of an eye, that room overflowed with tons of things that I had no need for, never used, and never thought about. Yes, it was caged, but it was a cluttered room filled with clutter just the same.

"And one day, when I caught myself wishing for an office, or a private getaway room, it finally occurred to me that one whole very important, very valuable room in our house was being used as a storage room for stuff I didn't care about. It was time to clutter-bust."

Are you wasting a whole room (that you could use in many different ways) just to store junk?

Some questions to ask about items in a spare room or other caged location:

- Has it worn out, stopped working, expired, or started to look ugly?
- For reading material, will I read or refer to it again?
- What if it is sentimental, but I don't love it? (I love the memory but not the item.) Can I keep the memory without the item?
- Do I want to continue to take care of this item and provide space for it?

DRESSERS AND CHESTS OF DRAWERS

Keep the tops as clear as possible. It's easier to dust, and the clutter-free look will encourage you to head off any stealth clutter that comes your way.

You probably have every shoe box and gift box you've ever received. Put them in the drawers to help keep items divided and not jumbled—socks in one, underwear in another, belts, scarves, pocket things in separate boxes. And, of course, put similar things together.

As much as is possible this time around, get rid of those greeting cards and other mementos that are taking up valuable space and not giving you any joy or delight because you never look at them.

China Cabinets and Other Furniture with Drawers

Now that you're cultivating some simple de-cluttering habits, take a look at these cages. You'll find many things that you never use and never will use. At Ron's house, for example, the china cabinet was his family's "Desperation Cage." When they couldn't find a good place to keep something and were desperate to stash it somewhere, they all seemed to turn to the china cabinet. When they went through it, they found old tablecloths that needed ironing but nobody would ever iron, wrinkled nonusable place mats, crunched-up wrapping paper, partly melted candles, and a bucket full of oddball items that should have been tossed out long ago.

The Garage

- Recruit friends or relatives.
- Before you start, have on hand trash bags and recycling bins, broom, dustpan, marking pen, shovel, bucket, string or twine to tie up old magazines, newspapers, or chunks of cardboard, a volunteer to schlep good stuff to the Salvation Army and bad stuff to the dump, something cool to drink, and snacks to sustain you and your helpers so you don't keel over.

- Decide ahead of time on a location for similar items like sports, camping, and garden equipment. You *did* plan to store such things together rather than scatter them all over the place, right?
- Do one small section at a time, even if you plan to work all day. (If you haul *everything* out to the driveway, then for some reason cannot finish the job, you'll dump everything back in and your time spent de-cluttering will have been wasted.)
- Move out cars, bikes, and any other big things.
- Before you start, dump everything that is obviously trash.
- Label boxes or bags: *donate, sell, toss,* or *repair.* Don't set up one for *not sure.* The time to decide is *now,* not later.
- As you fill each bag, take it to where it belongs and start a new one.
- Remember to group similar things together.
- Take care of big stuff first. Don't waste time sorting through all the different-sized screws. Just put all of them together for now and sort them later.
- When you box things up, make a label for each box; include a box number and a list of the contents. For example, "Box 1, Grandpa's Stuff: photos, baseball mitt, celebrity autograph collection." Or "Box 2, Taxes 2005," which is more specific than "Box 2, Taxes." (Be sure to tape the labels securely to the boxes, so they don't fall off.)
- Post a master list (Box 1, Grandpa's Stuff; Box 2, Taxes 2005, etc.) on the garage wall or in another location that

works for you. Now you won't have to drag everything out or paw through a gazillion boxes to find what you're searching for.

- Set up closely spaced shelves, which allow easy access to items. (With wide spaces between shelves, you end up with heavy, high stacks of stuff that have to be moved if you need what's at the bottom.)
- Long items such as brooms or shovels could hang from hooks on the wall, where they'll be easy to spot and free up floor space.

Once you're finished, sweep the floor if you want to. (You're decluttering today, so you may want to clean another day.) And consider doing one more purge. That's what Mahmood does after he's cleaned his garage and everything has a "happy home." As he explained, "I'll look at all the neat stacks to see if there are just three more things I can eliminate. And there always are." (He does the same thing after cleaning a closet. He goes back and sees if he can find just three more items to eliminate that are on shelves, floor, or hangers.)

THE WORKSHOP

- When cleaning the workshop, pull everything out. You'll spot duplicates, tools you've never used that are still in the boxes, and possibly realize that some items are missing (you loaned them to a few buddies) and now can request that they be returned.

- Get rid of what is broken or doesn't work anymore.
- Get rid of duplicates. If you sell duplicate tools at a garage sale or flea market, don't count on making big bucks.
- If you don't think you will need something soon, consider getting rid of it. *Or,* at least put it in a box, date it for a year from now, and if you don't use it in a year, give it away.
- Hang tools on a Peg-Board or slat board; then trace the outline of each tool on it. The use of outlines helps

not only you but also the rest of the family remember where to return tools; plus it lets you know what is missing.

- Have a handy portable toolcase stocked with necessities that you can carry to whatever job you're working on.
- Consider renting instead of owning big power tools that you'd hardly ever use.

Here's a tip from Erik: "I believe there is one instance where it's okay—even admirable—to have duplicates. My workshop is an unattached garage way in the back of our yard, and I am very reluctant to don mukluks and parka in the midst of a bone-chilling Chicago blizzard to trudge out there for a screwdriver. So I have treated myself to a duplicate hammer and screwdrivers—one regular and one Phillips head—to keep in a special spot in the house."

Now what about wood scraps? I'm married to a collector of all types and sizes of scraps of wood, which unfortunately attract critters that creep and crawl and go bump in the night. The only solution that works for me is to drag *all* the wood out, in order to sweep away dirt, nails, and creepy things. As we put the wood back, my husband will sometimes be willing to say good-bye to odd-shaped or ridiculously little pieces of wood. And sometimes not.

A "You've Got Clutter" Quiz

Are you storing items that are:

A. Rusted? (Your teen's rusty tricycle?)
B. Busted?
C. Water-damaged, moldy, mildewed?
D. Way too old to ever use?
E. Too unsafe to use? (Some old cribs, car seats, and playpens are considered downright dangerous.)
F. Beyond repair—ever?
G. Damaged by dirt, dust, cold, heat, or creepy crawly things?
H. All of the above?

If you answered yes to any of these questions, it's time to bite the bullet and start tossing.

THE ATTIC AND BASEMENT

Attics and basements are usually where we store the things that are big or sentimental or very expensive. The old computer, all kinds of camera equipment, china, crystal, heirlooms received, and heirlooms to pass on. Everything mentioned so far in this chapter also applies to attics and basements.

These tips are especially useful:

- Avoid blazing hot months for cleaning the attic. Choose dry days when you're hauling stuff outside of the garage, shed, or workshop.
- Store whatever you can in clear plastic boxes—sizes vary from smaller than a shoe box to larger than a laundry basket—so you can see what's inside without rummaging.
- Put holiday decorations (or anything used once a year or less) up above on rafters, if possible.

Charlie used to think that if he spent a lot of money for an item, he'd better keep it forever—whether it worked or not. Then one day his wife said something to him that changed his attitude toward clutter. "My wife wanted to throw out a computer that I bought long ago," he said, "and I didn't want to because it was so expensive when we bought it. She said that whether we got it for free or paid a million dollars for it, *it is still useless*. Keeping it for another century will not make it useful again."

STORAGE FACILITY

There may be times in your life when you need a storage facility temporarily. For example, if you've inherited a houseful of furniture, you may need time to sort through it, make decisions, and let others come and choose what they want.

But if you're thinking of storing stuff for the long haul, first determine if it truly means a *lot* to you. Do you really love, honor, and cherish this stuff? The amount of money you pay to store it for a year could be enough to cover the cost of some comforts in your life, such as a better car, a weekend away or an even longer vacation, or new furniture. It could be applied toward a college education for you or your children, or a more secure retirement, or improved medical or dental care that insurance does not cover. If you can afford to and choose to spend your money renting storage space, fine. But if it's going to cost money that you can't afford, use the clutter-busting tips in this book to help you keep only what you have enough room for, and dispose of the rest.

If, in spite of everything you've tried, you simply cannot let go of your accumulations but you want to, it may be time to consider professional counseling.

EXTRA CREDIT

My guess is that your top priorities to clear out are wild clutter spots. If you're working on those first, it will probably be quite a while before you're ready to start on your caged clutter. So this will be a simple assignment.

1. Make a list of all your caged clutter areas. That's it!

9

The Joy to Be Clutter-Free

He who would travel happily must travel light.
—Antoine de Saint-Exupéry

Perhaps you started this book feeling as if you were at war with clutter and you were losing the battle. Now you have hope, don't you?

Having a plan gives you hope. Being able to imagine yourself in control of your clutter gives you hope. Knowing that others (including me) have conquered their clutter, and that you can too, gives you hope.

Ramiro, a business owner, sent me an e-mail in which he reported how he was gaining control of the clutter in his life.

Dear Rita,
Last year, you gave a talk at our association about how clutter can take control of our lives, and I knew you were talking to me. Have you ever heard the Chinese proverb that says, "You don't own your possessions, they own you"? That happened to me.

As my business grew and I felt great success, I believed that meant I should buy everything I want, and beautiful, expensive jewelry for my wife and a wonderful new car.

Then we had to buy a new house to hold all the new things I bought, and a security system to protect everything, and I worried about people stealing my luxurious car. I became obsessed worrying about my things being stolen, broken, or wrecked by fire. My wife said I was making myself sick over it. My possessions owned my thoughts and my life.

A Native American guy told me he was raised with the saying, "Take all you need but take only what you need." My wife and I talked together and agreed that we had much too much more than we'd ever need and we didn't like the clutter everywhere in our lives. So after hearing your talk, I knew what to do.

I've stopped all my crazy spending sprees except for jewelry for my wife. She wants that to continue because she likes my taste.

And for a year, we've been giving away many, many things we did not need.

We still live a good life, a great life, but the clutter that covered everything has started to wither and soon will be under control. Things are very much better.

Rita, you have a good message for business and for life. Keep preaching it.

Ramiro is absolutely right. The more possessions you have, the more you have to make room for, take care of, protect, sometimes insure, and sometimes worry about losing them to theft, fire, or other catastrophes. Yet when you start to get rid of your unneeded possessions, you can rejoice in a newfound freedom, for you are no longer "owned" by all your possessions.

Furthermore, when you finally are rid of the clutter in your life, it becomes amazingly easy for you to be organized and efficient.

- You can find what you're looking for.
- You can use a desktop or table or floor or counter for what it's supposed to be used for.
- You can work much more easily.
- You don't lose things or lose track of what you want to do.
- You can focus and pay attention more easily and successfully.
- You can work on one thing at a time because there's room to work on it.
- You can actually write a list of things you want to do because you can find paper to write on, and you have space to set the paper on while writing. (Plus you won't automatically lose the list because you have designated a place to keep it.)
- You don't have to call in the National Guard to start a search every time you need a pen to write your list

To be clutter-free gives you not only more physical space but also more emotional space. When you are surrounded by confusion, you feel confused; when you are surrounded by junk, you feel junky. Clutter can sabotage goals and dreams. There is a definite connection between clutter and a person's feelings of self-worth. Because you made the decision to gain control of your clutter, you're no longer embarrassed by it or feel like a messy, disorganized loser. Instead, you feel like a successful, achieving winner.

Revel in it. Let yourself be happy, delighted, and proud of your new clutter-free life. Every time you look at your clean, neat room, office, desk, car, drawer, floor, or whatever, affirm and lock in your new status as a Clutter Buster. Out loud or to yourself, say something that makes you feel proud of your achievement.

Celebrate your success. Even if you cleared away only one small, tiny area of clutter, that is a success. Celebrate.

WILL CLUTTER EVER RETURN?

Yes, there will be times when some of your clutter will return—maybe because of sickness or crisis in your life, or a superbusy time, or overnight guests, or anything else that keeps you from following your usual routine. But the clutter will never be as bad as it was. If you've cultivated such simple habits as "A place for everything, and everything in its place" and "Feed your wastebasket," you'll be doing clutter prevention without even trying.

When clutter does start to accumulate again, don't beat yourself up. You're human. Look back through some of the chapters in this book to recharge your battery. If there are certain habits or tips you want to incorporate into your lifestyle, write them out and post them on the bathroom mirror, refrigerator, above your desk, or some other place where you will see them frequently.

Also, observe what is starting to become clutter and see if you can either find places to put that stuff or develop a system to keep it under control. According to Mark Victor Hansen, co-author of the *Chicken Soup for the Soul* series, systems are enormously important because they enable you to:

Save
Your
Self
Time
Energy and
Money

Terry, for example, discovered that some of the paper clutter accumulating in his house was vacation brochures. He realized that he was stacking them on the counter as if they were short-term items he was going to read over and toss. But he wasn't tossing them because he hoped that he and his wife, Traci, could travel to these places someday. Finally, he set up a vacation file in the same file cabinet where he kept bills and insurance documents. That location might not seem logical to you, but it has worked for him. Now he reads over the brochures, shows them to Traci, then files them away. No clutter.

Here's the clutter-prevention system I use when papers start to stack up on my desk (especially after I've been out of town for three weeks or more). I label several folders (e.g., "Clients," "Letters," "Proposals," "Teleseminars," "To Be Filed," "To Act On") and put each paper in the correct folder. That way, if I have to rifle through a stack searching for a letter, I may have to plow through a bunch of letters, but at least I'm not rummaging through every single paper on my desk.

THE NEW AND IMPROVED YOU

As you start to see your clutter evaporate, you'll notice changes occurring in your life. A lot of your stress melts away, and you start to feel different—better, happier, even healthier.

You will also notice a change in your priorities, which enables you to reduce your "social clutter." That is, you no longer

---

FIVE EASY RULES TO KEEP CLUTTER AT BAY

We live in a world of incoming clutter. No, we don't have to become obsessive or compulsive about clutter-busting, but just follow a few easy rules:

1. Regularly get rid of items that are no longer useful.
2. Think twice before bringing something into our home.
3. Find a place for all our stuff to live.
4. Immediately put things where they belong instead of setting them down "to put away later."
5. Have a simple few habits and systems in place.

That's the way to keep the clutter at bay and from overrunning our living and work spaces and from overwhelming our lives.

---

spend time with people, groups, organizations, volunteer work, and activities that aren't meaningful or important to you anymore.

Each step you take in discarding or preventing your clutter leads you to a greater sense of freedom. Eliminating clutter from your life gives you a wonderful feeling of ease. You'll start to feel more in control of your life, with more energy and a glorious sense of satisfaction.

You may even notice a skip in your step as you journey through life without having to drag along all that clutter.

A "You've Got Clutter" Quiz

As you become a Clutter Conqueror, how can you get ideas to organize what's left?

A. Ask friends ("How do you store spools of thread or odd-shaped ice cream sundae dishes?" "What is your best tip for organizing an office?")

B. Read tips—in magazines, newspapers, and on the Internet.

C. Check out the container sections of stores, especially office supply stores.

D. Read a book on getting organized. (This suggestion is not for everyone. Some people prefer to pick up only one tip at a time.)

E. Watch TV shows that focus on clutter-busting and organizing places.

Whether you decide to follow any of these suggestions doesn't matter; you're a winner. You have finished this book, and even if you haven't started to clutter-bust yet, you will. You won't be able to *not* tackle your clutter, because reading this book shatters some of your Clutter Numbness. Things you used to ignore will now start to bug you. You have all the ideas, tips, and solutions you need.

~~~~~~~~~~~~~~~~~~~~~~~~~~~~

When your clutter starts to evaporate, you'll discover more space, more time, and that you can find what you need when you need it. As a result, you'll feel lighter, more energized, more organized (finally!), and more like a winner.

As you become more organized, you'll lose that self-image of being scatterbrained or flaky. You'll see subtle changes in your relationships (fewer complaints from people you live with, fewer put-downs from outsiders), and you'll be more efficient and productive at work. Some people even observe a change in their posture. They describe it as "walking taller in both body and soul."

All this because when you look around, what do you see?

KA-BOOM! No more clutter.

Acknowledgments

❖

Being an author is more fun than I ever imagined. If you have a book in your heart, you've *got* to write it; you never know what will happen. For me, being a published author is a dream come true.

It's also incredible how much work and help from others is needed to turn ideas into a book that makes sense. Although the author gets all the credit for writing a book, no book is ever complete without the help, kindness, and generosity of many people.

A whole gang of people deserve a round of applause for this clutter-busting book, too many to mention here. But I couldn't live with myself if I didn't at least thank a few wonderful souls.

Most happy authors have a "trinity" of hardworking people: the publisher, the editor, and the agent. I'm no exception.

My deepest gratitude goes to George Gibson, a champion and a gentleman among publishers. Without his kindness and support for me and the promotion of our books, nobody would even know they exist.

I am enormously grateful to my editor, Jackie Johnson, who suggested I write about clutter. She organizes my disorganized thoughts, smoothes out my rough edges, can always come up with the right word or phrase when we need it, and gently prods me to create the illusion that I am a professional writer. I appreciate her understanding, intelligence, and toughness. Just what I need.

A very special thank-you to my new agent, Danielle Egan-Miller, who stepped in when my much-loved agent, Jane Jordan Browne, passed away. Jane's was a tough role to fill, but Danielle displays the same enthusiasm, caring, work ethic, and savvy that Jane possessed. Danielle always has time for me, and her moral support and friendship go well beyond the job of an agent.

I am grateful to many others, including: Mickey Forster, my Web goddess and niece, who created my awesome Web site; Ruth Coleman, for helping to move me along when I was stuck and for her wisdom, vision, and, most of all, friendship; Jo-Anne Knight, for assisting me with hoarding—no, I mean with information on hoarding—and in so many other ways; Maureen Edgar, Linda Brakeall, Carolyn (C. J.) Jonasen, and Mike Wynne, for their willingness to read drafts of this book and for their ideas when my brain was turning to mush; and Doris Payne and Orla Clancy, for their creative and unusual concepts of clutter.

A special thank-you to Meg and John Gleeson for their hilarious and very human story. Unfortunately, I'm not allowed to tell you which story is theirs.

Heartfelt thanks and a hug and a smooch to all of you who buy and read my books. You amaze and thrill me.

To all my family and friends: I appreciate your words of encouragement, and your patience when I disappear for weeks at a time to hole up in my office writing to meet deadlines. Also, thanks to those of you who, when you come upon my books in bookstores, turn them face-out for everyone to see.

In the acknowledgment sections of my other books, I noted that my husband, Bruce, hadn't read them—not one single word. He still hasn't read them. Whenever I call him on it, he quietly, calmly reminds me that there are many ways for a husband to support his wife. Reading her books is *not* the only way. Then he goes on to remind me that he *does* read the acknowledgments . . . to be sure that he's included. Since I'm a happy woman who loves life, the guy must be doing something right.

Everyone mentioned here (and I apologize to those I overlooked) has played an important part in my life's journey and this book. I am so grateful and so blessed. Thank you and God bless you all.

Index

Act stack, 116–18
Albums
  keepsake, 66
  photo, 50–52
Animal shelters, 59
Attic, 167–68
Auctions.yahoo.com, selling on, 57

Baby furniture, 34–35
Bargains, 104–6
Basement, 167–68
Bathroom, 141
Beauty salons, 67
Bed, extra, 148
Bedrooms, 140–41
Big stuff first, 163
Binders, 113
Books, 126
Boundaries, setting, 22, 24

Boxes, labels for, 22, 74–75, 163
Buddies, help from, 67–68, 75, 76, 158
Bulletin boards, flyers on, 56
Business cards, 128–29
Business clothing, 65
Business-related clutter, 23–24

Caged clutter, 10–13, 154–70
  in attic and basement, 167–68
  in chests and dressers, 161–62
  in closets, 155–59
  in drawers, 161–62
  in the garage, 162–64
  in glove compartments, 159–60
  listing, 170
  quiz, 167
  in a spare room, 160–61
  in storage facilities, 168–69

Caged clutter *(continued)*
  temporary, 155
  in the workshop, 164–66
Careers, switching, 23
Caregivers, 22, 25
Catalogs, 125–26
Chaos, 17
Charge cards, 104
Child-care centers, 67
Childhood, memories of, 37
Children
  clutter-busters, 143–50
  leaving clutter behind when
    leaving home, 99
  party gifts to, 49
  school papers of, 129–30
Circle of Couch Giving, 55–56
Classified ads, 56
Closets, 91–92, 155–59
Clothes
  business, 65
  in closets, 91–92, 155–59
  donating, 65
  hand-me-downs, 66
  how often you wear, 158
  for rummage sales, 66
  seasonal sorting, 96, 159
  to secondhand store, 66
Clothes hampers, 93, 140
Clutter
  begets clutter, 78
  business-related, 23–24

caged vs. wild, 10–13
covering up, 155
definition of, 5
five rules for, 176
returning, 88, 174–76
professions that promote,
  23–24
tame, 14–15
Clutter Conqueror, 178
Clutter Cop, 106–7, 136–37
Clutter Culprit, 97–100
Clutter Facts
  chaos, 17
  getting organized, 4
  getting rid of mementos, 38
  a place for everything, 7
Clutter generation, 6–9
Clutter Glutton, 16
Clutter numbness, 16, 29, 178
Clutterers, 15–26
  Caregivers, 22, 25
  Clutter Glutton, 16
  Compulsive Hoarders, 16*n*
  Crusader Collector, 20
  Duplicator, 20
  Hobbyist, 21–22
  Pack Rat, 17–18
  Parent Curator, 26
  Receiver, 19
  Shopper, 18
Clutter-free, joy of being,
  171–80

Collections
    announcing the end of, 43
    breaking the habit of, 39
    as clutter, 39–44
    decisions about, 39
    display of, 40, 41, 42, 43
    evaluating, 52
    as investments, 43
    as legacy, 43
    magnificent obsession of,
        41–43
    as memories, 38
    organization of, 42
    packing away, 41
    of photos, 50–52
    questions about, 42
    storage of, 42
    valuable, 43–44
Comparison-shopping, 104
Compulsive Hoarders, 16n
Computers, 130–34
    cybercards via, 128
    getting rid of, 57–58
    message boards on, 57
    selling via, 57
Control, 11–12, 50, 175
Cosmetics, tossing out, 142
Craft projects, donating items for,
        66, 67, 128, 141
Crusader Collector, 20
Crutches, 64
Cybercards, 128

Decisions, making, 39, 56,
        68–69, 86–87, 100, 110, 134
Decorations, holiday, 105–6, 168
Deprivation, fear of, 27–28
Dining room, 141
Dining-room-table file system, 5
Display
    of collections, 40, 41, 42, 43
    of jewelry, 92–93
    of mementos, 38, 40
Disposal, safe, 61
Divorced friends, donations for,
        62
Doctors' offices, 59, 67
Doll Lady, 40
Donations, 58–60, 80
    calling first, 58
    by Caregiver, 22
    by children, 150
    Circle of Couch Giving, 55–56
    containers for, 61
    creative, 61, 68
    of food items, 96
    for fund-raisers, 58
    of gifts, 48, 49
    memories of loved ones, 38
    organizations that receive, 59
    quality items for, 63
    tools, 62
    visualizing, 28
Downsizing, 27, 36
Dressers/drawers, 161–62

Dump runs, 64
Dumpster rental, 64
Duplicator, 20, 142, 164

eBay.com, selling on, 57
Edges, attacking first, 75
Empty space, 141
End of clutter, announcing, 43
Entry area, 140
Estate sales, 57
Exchange, 58
Exhaustion, plateau of, 14

Family heirlooms, 65
Family photos, 65
Family room, 141
Family service centers, 61
Files, 5, 111, 112–16, 135
First house, donations for, 62
First time hardest, 77–80
Flea markets, 57
Flyers on bulletin boards, 56
Focus, 71, 73
Folders, 175–76
Food pantry, 62, 96
Foster homes, 59
Freecycle.org, message boards, 57
Freedom, 177
Friends, help from, 67–68, 75,
    76, 158

Fund-raisers, 58, 124
Furniture
    baby, 34–35
    tops of, 141, 161

Garage, 162–64
Garage sales, 56–57, 61, 80
Garbage dump, 64
Gifts, 44–47
    communication about,
        46–47
    control over, 50
    getting rid of, 38, 44, 48, 49
    party, 48–50
    rationalization, 45
    suggestions for, 46–47
Give it away, 62
Glove compartment, 159–60
Goodwill Industries, 59
Great Results newsletter, 6
Greeting cards, 127–28
Grouping similar items, 80–81,
    112, 138, 142, 159, 163

Habitat for Humanity, 62
Habits
    breaking, 39, 104
    building, 83, 85, 111,
        136–38
    scheduling, 95–97

Hampers, clothes, 93, 140
Hand-me-downs, 66
Heirlooms, family, 65
Hell drawer, 14–15, 91
Hobbyist, 21–22, 154
Holiday decorations, 105–6,
     168
Hospitals, 59, 67
Hunt, thrill of, 40

Information overload, 109,
     133–34
Inherited mementos, 31–33
Investments, collections as, 43

Jewelry, display of, 92–93
Jewelry boxes, 78–80
Jobs, tools for, 23–24

Keepsake albums, 66
Kitchen, 138–40
   counter space in, 80, 83,
     138–39
   hell drawer in, 14–15, 91
   Murphy's Law of, 139–40

Labels, 22, 74–75, 163
Legacy, collections as, 43

Letting go, 26–28
Libraries, donations to, 59, 61,
     67, 126
Lifestyle, of clutter, 9
Lindbergh, Anne Morrow, 41
Living room, 141
Lockbox, 119

Magazines, 67, 96, 111,
     121–25
Mail and messages, 111, 120,
     131–32
Master list, 163–64
Matching similar items, 80–81,
     112, 138, 142, 159, 163
Mementos, 26, 31–36
   baby furniture, 34–35
   clothing, 159
   display of, 38, 40
   getting ready to say good-bye
     to, 33–34, 38
   inherited, 31–33
   keepsake albums, 66
   passing them on, 34
   photos of, 51
   quiz, 35–36
Memories, 26, 28, 36–38
   of childhood, 37
   of loved ones, 38
Memory Box, 37
Mental exercises, 28–30

Message boards, 57
Messages and mail, 111, 120,
    131–32
Multitasking, 71
Murphy's Law of the Kitchen,
    139–40
Museum, leaving it in, 47–48

Newlyweds, giving tools to, 62
Notes, 126–27
Numbness, clutter, 16, 29, 178
Nursing homes
  donating items to, 59, 67,
    141
  move to, 44

Odds and ends, 89
Off-season items, 82
Organization, 4, 178
Organizations, donations to,
    59

Pack Rats, 17–18
Pantry, clearing out, 96
Paper, 109–35
  act stack, 116–18
  books, 126
  business cards, 128–29
  catalogs, 125–26
  from child's school, 129–30
  computer, 130–34
  file stack, 112–16, 135
  folders for, 175–76
  greeting cards, 127–28
  handling once, 100, 111, 134
  information overload, 109,
    133–34
  magazines, 121–25
  mail and messages, 111, 120,
    131–32
  notes, 126–27
  ordinary clutter, 110–21
  in safety deposit box, 119
  stand and deliver, 118–19
  time-wasting, 117
  toss stack, 119–21, 135
Parent Curator, 26
Party gifts, 48–50
Pass it on, 34
Pegboard, 165–66
Photos
  before and after, 152
  dating and sorting, 51
  discarding lesser quality, 50
  for family members, 65
  keepsake albums, 66
  of mementos, 51
  organizing, 50–52
  storing, 51
Place for everything, 4, 7, 82, 87,
    137, 174

Poker night, 58
Possessions
  being owned by, 172
  identity via, 8
Procrastination, 13–14, 89–90,
    100–101, 115
  do it now, 7, 30, 111
Professional clutter, 23–24
Purse, clutter in, 91, 97

Quilting guilds, 59
Quizzes
  bringing in more clutter, 25
  holding on to items, 10
  magazines, 122
  mementos, 35–36
  organization, 178
  starting out, 84
  storage, 167

Rationalization, 17–18, 45
Receiver, 19
Recycling, 75–77
Religious organizations, 59, 61, 62
Removals, 82
Repair vs. replacement, 8
Retrieval, 9, 111, 114
Rewards, 73, 86
Rummage sales, 57, 66, 117
Rummaging, 90–93

Safe disposal, 61
Safety deposit box, 119
Salvation Army, 59
Saying no, 28
Schedule, 87, 95–97
Schools
  craft materials for, 66, 67, 128,
    141
  donations to, 59
  fund-raisers, 124
Select one area, 71, 86, 163
Self-employment, 23–24
Self-image, 180
Selling your clutter, 28, 56–58
Senior centers, magazines for,
    67
Shadow box frames, 38
Shelters, 59, 61
Shopper, 18, 101–6, 107–8, 156,
    159
Silent auctions, 59
SINS, deadly, 4
SMART strategy, 80–83
Space, empty, 141
Spare room, 160–61
Stand and deliver, 89, 118–19
Starting out, 70–87
  attack edges first, 75
  big stuff first, 163
  budgeting five minutes for,
    74
  building habits, 83, 85

Starting out *(continued)*
  choosing where to start, 83, 86,
    137–38
  decisions, 74, 76–77, 83, 86,
    137–38
  donations, 80
  first time hardest for, 77–80
  focus, 71, 73
  get friend to help, 75, 76
  grouping similar items, 80–81
  label boxes, 74–75
  a place for everything, 82, 87
  quiz, 84
  recycle, 75–77
  regular schedule, 87
  reward, 73, 86
  select one area, 71, 86, 163
  SMART strategy, 80–83
  START smart, 74–77
  STING, 71, 73
  storage, 80
  timer set for, 71, 73
  toss, 75–77, 82
Stealth clutter, 88–108
  Clutter Cop vs., 106–7
  odds and ends, 89
  procrastination, 89–90,
    100–101
  returning, 88, 174–76
  rummaging, 90–93
  schedule, 95–97

  shopping, 101–6, 107–8
  from someone else,
    97–100
  too busy, 93–95
STING, 71, 73
Storage
  of caged clutter, 11–12, 80
  of collections, 42
  creative, 151
  of off-season items, 82
  of photos, 51
  quiz, 167
  in safe deposit box, 119
  temporary, 98, 112
Storage units, paying for, 27,
  168–69
Stress management, 101–2
Suitcase, how to pack, 92
System, developing, 174–75

Tablecloth, covering clutter with,
  155
Tame clutter, 14–15
Tax papers, 110–11, 114–16
Tech stuff, selling, 57–58
Theater groups, 59, 62
Theme displays, 38, 50
Three-day waiting period,
  104
Thrift shops, 59

Thrill of the hunt, 40
Throw stuff away, 64
Time, pockets of, 137
    five minutes a day, 74
Timer, setting, 71, 73, 93–95
Tools
    duplicate, 165, 166
    giving away, 62
    pegboard for, 165–66
    professional, 23–24
    renting, 166
    workshop, 164–66
Toss it out, 75–77, 82, 97, 99, 119–21, 135
Trading your things, 58
Trash, discards in, 64

Usefulness, 8

Valuable collections, 43–44
Veterans' groups, 59, 60
Visualization, 28

Wastebaskets, 93–94, 120–21, 140, 174
Where will I put this?, 13–14, 19
Wild clutter, 10–13
Will I keep this?, 13
Wood scraps, 166
Workshop, 164–66

Yard sales, 62
Year, time limit before disposal, 64, 67, 165
You, new and improved, 176–80

If you have thoughts or comments about this book, would like to share your clutter story, or would like information about other products and services offered by Rita Emmett, contact her at her
Web site

www.RitaEmmett.com
E-mail: Rita@RitaEmmett.com

or at

Emmett Enterprises, Inc.
2331 Eastview Drive
Des Plaines, IL 60018